IF BY MAGIC

THE WORDS AND LORE OF THE GIROBABIES

BY
MARK MCGHEE

2008-2025

Salamander Street

First published in 2025 by Salamander Street Ltd.
(info@salamanderstreet.com)

Copyright © Mark McGhee 2025

Mark McGhee has asserted his right to be identified as the author of this Work in accordance with the Copyright, Designs and Patents Act 1988.

You may not copy, store, distribute, transmit, reproduce or otherwise make available this publication (or any part of it) in any form, or binding or by any means (print, electronic, digital, optical, mechanical, photocopying, recording or otherwise), without the prior written permission of the publisher. Any person who does any unauthorised act in relation to this publication may be liable to criminal prosecution and civil claims for damages.

A CIP catalogue record for this book is available from the British Library.

Cover design by Shona Skylar

Social Not Working album cover design by Jerry Dowds

Bustop Apocalypse album cover design by Shona Skylar

Who Stole Utopia? album cover design by Martyn Yeun

Dreams are Mental album cover design by Shona Skylar

Thanks to the photographers whose work appears in the montages especially Martin Windebank.

ISBN: 9781068233470

10 9 8 7 6 5 4 3 2 1

Introduction

I'm not sure where these words even come from. It's as if they magically appear from some sort of unknown source. During a time of grief, illness and hedonism both myself and my friend John Hayes's contracts were terminated from a call centre in Glasgow. We had talked about starting a band together and so we started to record multiple demos every day using an old PC, an acoustic guitar belonging to my father, and a cheap microphone designed for a PlayStation karaoke game. We would drink, smoke and upload one-take demos to a now obsolete website called Myspace and, before we knew it, my friend Martyn Yuen joined on bass and we found a French drummer called Claude by him putting up an advert on a board at Carlton Studios in the Gorbals. It seems like a lifetime ago now with the world unrecognisable to what it was when we started but I think the last album that we released—*Dreams are Mental*—in 2025 was the perfect way to end the story of the band. Every day I would cast the net out to fish for words and, as if by magic, they appeared by the barrel-load more often than not. I have boxes and boxes of them everywhere and became obsessed with making rhymes about everything from social commentary to psychobabble.

Every song we started with a fresh page and were never confined by genre or mood. We made rock, we made punk, we made techno, we made folk, we made hip-hop. We made serious records and we made completely daft, silly stuff. We eventually went on to play these songs live to a sold-out Barrowland Ballroom, festival stages up and down the country, and shared bills with some of our heroes. We would record around five albums' worth of songs, the majority of which will be shared within these pages. As I looked back on them during the process, it felt like flicking through an old book of photographs. So many memories trapped in sound and scribbled notebooks. I can see where I improved and when I overcomplicated things. The sweet spot is to keep it direct but leave it open to interpretation, and sometimes I succeeded in doing that. Leonard Cohen once said "If I knew where the good songs were, I'd go there more often."

I have interviewed, collaborated with and even drank with thousands of artists and nobody has ever given me a straight answer about where they get their ideas from. I think history will remember our generation as low-IQ prehistoric creatures that seemed to tap into something otherly from time to time and made something out of nothing that created all ranges of reactions and emotions from complete strangers.

When I am naming my albums, I have a good idea of the concept and I try to let the concept inform the name and not the other way around. During the process there are always three words that ascend off the page and instantly dictate the rest of the project. It's always three words for some reason, and I am not sure why that is. When compiling this book, the words 'If By Magic' danced off the page while I was adding notes to a song called *Late Night Sketchy,* and that halted the decision-making process of what to call this book in its tracks. You have probably never heard of *The Girobabies* outside of Glasgow because our tours were never normally well-attended. We were completely DIY, with no management, no label, no booker, no sponsored ads, no radio plugger, no team, no contacts, no friends within the industry and no—as in ZERO—budget. As well as being the only surviving member of the original line up of *The Girobabies*, I have also released three hip-hop albums under the name *Jackal Trades*, I am a spoken-word poet called Mark McG (previously Mark Mywords until I found out that name was not the unique thought that I thought it was), I host a podcast and YouTube channel called *You Call That Radio*, and I am a promoter, manager, booker, songwriter and producer for other bands. As well as being a curator, programmer, artist liaison, stage manager and booker for events and music festivals. None of those things would have happened without being sacked from my job on the same day as Hazy.

This book is dedicated to everybody who helped me along the way, the doors that miraculously opened up and the adventures these songs have taken me on. As if by magic.

Mark McGhee
2025

Acknowledgements

I would like to thank all my friends and family for their support. And all band members past and present. There are probably over 60 names that should be on this list but I am scared I will miss someone out so thank you ALL, but especially John Hayes, Martyn Yuen, Robbie Gunn, Jo D'arc, Gordy Duncan and Mark McKeown. All the album artwork was compiled by a myriad of Martyn Yuen, George Glen and Jerry Dowds. The book artwork was compiled by Shona Skylar. Thanks for feedback from Doctur Normul and thanks for the support from Dougie O' Neil.

I would like to thank Martin Windebank for being the first person to answer the call when we needed a music video and Thomas Adams for taking us out on the road countless times.

I would like to thank Morphamish at Sound Sound studios for bringing our most recent album *Dreams Are Mental* to life. And thank you to Paul McCabe for turning our last two albums into vinyl.

I would also like to thank Lucy at Salamander Street for taking a chance on me to print my first book of words.

Thanks to the lady who sacked me.

And finally, thank you to anyone else who has supported us throughout the years. You are very much appreciated more than you will ever know.

All the following songs should be available on Bandcamp and most streaming sites.

Linktr.ee/Girobabies to follow us on socials.

Contents

CHAPTER ONE: SOCIAL NOT WORKING

Backlash	2
What Could Go Wrong?	5
Stalker Drama	7
Bank Charge	10
Time Machine Prescription	13
Jeremy Kyle	15
Liquid Sky	17
Party Around Me	19

CHAPTER TWO: BUS STOP APOCALYPSE

What Victor Said	24
Overheard in the Westend	25
Nightmare	27
Countdown to Tinnitus	29
Idiot's Guide to Karma	31
Shonzo the Security Guard	33
I Want Answers	35
Drip Effect	37
The Giros	40
Big Society	43
Fluffy Puppy Rainbow Flower	45

CHAPTER THREE: WHO TOOK UTOPIA?

Equinox	50
Secret Animal	51
Mirroshow	54
Brain Rocket (and the evolution of turtles)	55
Late Night Sketchy	57
Bring Potions	59
Planet Fort Knox	62
No Place Like No Place	65
Ramp up the Theatre	67
Escape! Routine!	70
Short interlude	76

CHAPTER FOUR: DREAMS ARE MENTAL

We Need An Intro	80
Landfill Culture	81
The Secret Information	84
Ordinary Day (3:33am)	88
Her Fancy Man	91
Foggy Windows	93
The Catch	96
It Felt Like The End	99
This Not Circus	102
Steal My Sleep	105
Fat Elvis Time	107
A Light at Glasgow Central	109

THE GIROBABIES — 113

CHAPTER ONE:
SOCIAL NOT WORKING

2010

BACKLASH

Insecurity
The root of the lunacy
Cardboard cutouts cutting through the community
Tracksuit terrorists on the terraces
Petty crime menaces
The wannabe Paulferrises
It's serious how the IQ has dropped
In the last five years by such a fucking lot
Claiming to be gangsters when they're clearly not
I sincerely hope every one of thems shot

From the street young team to the club drug scene
And it's not just me we'll be going full-teamed
Full steam where victims laugh as the demons scream
And karma will wake up
It's the backlash dream

Opportunity
The root of the lunacy
Governing bodies and the social security
Pen-pushing Nazis in their matching Versaces
Expensive Christmas parties paid by taxes and charges
It's serious how voter apathy has won
In the last ten years we've been overrun
PR-spun with a smoking gun
Politics seems pointless and narcotics more fun
And it's not just me that is thinking like this
No definition of democracy has ever existed

Full steam where victims laugh
As the demons scream
And karma will wake up
It's the backlash dream

> Take the streets back
> Take the streets back
> Take the streets back

We'll have a backlash if you want tay
Let's up the ante
The good guy gets mad he's a bad vigilante
Rise up or do nante
Whatever you want tay

Backlash at last
Take the streets back
Rob the banks and the SAAS
Take the streets back
Watch the stockmarkets crash
Take the streets back
Burn the stash and the cash
Take the streets back
The psycopaths are at large
Take the streets back
Deport all racists and laugh
Take the streets back
Let the good guy laugh last
Take the streets back

I remember leaving the booth to see the rest of the band staring at me with what in hindsight was a look of fear. It was my first time even being in a recording studio. Vocals were at the end so I had hours and hours to pluck up some Dutch courage by drinking lots of beer. By the time it was my shot, the music was really loud in my headphones. I didn't know you could choose volume so I shouted very loud and very out of tune, scaring everyone who was outside the booth with my 'passion', as they politely agreed that I should maybe give it another shot. Like most of the early songs, Backlash *was written live as Hazy picked away at a giant, ancient acoustic guitar that we borrowed off my Dad. All songs were initially recorded in one take and uploaded to the internet. The only thing mixed about the first takes was the response. We had both just lost our jobs and getting our first proper taste of what the media at that time called 'the credit crunch'. I think the first song was called* Smoking Ban *but we must have made about 100 tracks in those days with varying results. This one became far more powerful once we added bass and drums into the mix and ended up being the first song on* Social Not Working, *and also our opening song for most shows we played in the early years. thewisegoldfish would also remix this song, which became a theme song for my podcast* You Call That Radio *during the lockdown era.*

WHAT COULD GO WRONG?

Stabbed in the back, hit with the sack
The social not working, kicked out your flat
Under arrest, under attack
Walk under a ladder with a magpie and a cat
Tug-of-war tussle with the mental muscle
Must muster something above the lacklustre

Such is life, stick a grin on it

What could possibly go wrong?—Everything
What could possibly go wrong?—Anything
What could possibly go wrong?—Everything
Every day is a Friday the 13th
The rage from within, the lies and the spin
What could possibly go wrong?—Everything

We burnt the bridge—It hit the skids and we're glad it did
Such is life, stick a grin on it

I remember leaving the booth to see the rest of the band staring at me with what in hindsight was a look of fear. It was my first time even being in a recording studio. Vocals were at the end so I had hours and hours to pluck up some Dutch courage by drinking lots of beer. By the time it was my shot, the music was really loud in my headphones. I didn't know you could choose volume so I shouted very loud and very out of tune, scaring everyone who was outside the booth with my 'passion', as they politely agreed that I should maybe give it another shot. Like most of the early songs, Backlash *was written live as Hazy picked away at a giant, ancient acoustic guitar that we borrowed off my Dad. All songs were initially recorded in one take and uploaded to the internet. The only thing mixed about the first takes was the response. We had both just lost our jobs and getting our first proper taste of what the media at that time called 'the credit crunch'. I think the first song was called* Smoking Ban *but we must have made about 100 tracks in those days with varying results. This one became far more powerful once we added bass and drums into the mix and ended up being the first song on* Social Not Working, *and also our opening song for most shows we played in the early years. thewisegoldfish would also remix this song, which became a theme song for my podcast* You Call That Radio *during the lockdown era.*

WHAT COULD GO WRONG?

Stabbed in the back, hit with the sack
The social not working, kicked out your flat
Under arrest, under attack
Walk under a ladder with a magpie and a cat
Tug-of-war tussle with the mental muscle
Must muster something above the lacklustre

Such is life, stick a grin on it

What could possibly go wrong?—Everything
What could possibly go wrong?—Anything
What could possibly go wrong?—Everything
Every day is a Friday the 13th
The rage from within, the lies and the spin
What could possibly go wrong?—Everything

We burnt the bridge—It hit the skids and we're glad it did
Such is life, stick a grin on it

The lyrics 'such is life' and 'stick a grin on it' were phrases my Dad used to say a lot. And 'what could go wrong' became a sort of inside joke as everything around us was regularly turning to shit for reasons within and outwith our control. This was the first song we ever wrote as part of an actual band in a rehearsal studio. As well as bass and drums, we also welcomed a second guitarist called Robbie Gunn who would become more pivotal as the years passed, but he really kicked this idea off with a riff that reminds me of an old Sega computer game called Alex Kidd. *It was also given a techno remix by Sicknote who I sometimes joined onstage during their Scottish shows, and that version still gets played in nightclubs and festivals across Europe. The original verison has a music video which was one of my first forays into video editing and features footage of myself and Hazy getting beat 16-0 in a football match for our friend Fergie. Shout out to Brendan for rigging the game by putting healthy pub football players and even a semi-pro in the team to play against heavy smokers and drinkers. We finished the game with 13 players and even missed a penalty.*

STALKER DRAMA

You can find her
disguised as a passing dog walker
in a stalker submarine with binoculars
or a helicopter
sifting through wheelie bins for credit cards and love letters
vengeance vendetta and a hidden agenda
ulterior motive and a hidden agenda
all communications returned back to sender
you reap what you sow so you drove me to this
I'm not a psychologist
not your psychiatrist
Jack and Jill went up the hill to fetch a pale of water
she's got a needle and she's not on the pill because somebody caught her
it's good to stalk
a stalker
God call the doctor
Completely off her rocker
There Lies the Stalker

    we're gonna be married
    we're gonna be happy

creepy sneaky peeker peering through the curtains, oh!
wide-angled camera
sidestep all the karma
wide-angled camera
focus on the stalker drama

voodoo dolls and the darkest form of magic
hair in her purse and a lab in her attic
playing games of chess with her vague empty threats
give her an address and she'll open her legs
smoking your ashtray

drinking your dregs
behind you in the queue every time you got to Gregg`s
the nutter's got your number
your phone and your pin
the police are good for nothing they just play the violin

it's good to stalk a stalker
God call the doctor
shock, horror, shocker
the karma of the drama stalker

I don't want to reveal too much generally about what the lyrics mean to me as I think art should be about what the reader or listener makes of it but I definitely don't want to get into this one for obvious reasons. All I can say is this was based on two true stories. It was also the first time we welcomed Jess Hopkins into the fold. Because of the lyrics 'the police are good for nothing they just play the violin' I thought it would be good to add a new dimension to the song and we had jammed with Jess before. I asked her to do something that sounded like a cross between Jaws *and* Psycho *and she totally nailed it first time.*

The first draft of this was written before I had another band member. I worked in a call centre and despite the fact I was getting paid reasonably well on a weekly basis I would usually be skint the day before payday. The bank I was with had a system whereby I was allowed to go over by up to £10 without getting any bank charges so this would sometimes cover food or beer costs on a Thursday. Overnight, that system changed and it would mean that one measly onion made me go over by 16 pence on the 18th October to which the bank wanted £35 for said onion. While I was complaining I made sure my wages went into another account, to which I became aware they were charging me £100 per month for one bloody onion for over a year. I gave up arguing and just ignored the letters until I was sent a letter saying I owed £1,732.55p for one fucking onion. A year or so later once the band had started jamming, I was called by a debt collector who said if I paid £700 today they would wipe the debt. I thanked them for the kind offer but politely declined it. It then made me finish the song and I also performed it as a poem many times over the years. Although parts have dated, it has maintained a longevity by changing certain words and having the audience join in for the chorus.

TIME MACHINE PRESCRIPTION

And he prescribed me
a time machine
was at the doctor's as part of my dream
And he prescribed me
a time machine
with a magic watch on his wrist with a laserbeam
Oh no he says there's no way back for you
unless you go back in time you can't rewind with your mind

If you're quick you will witness my descent and then
you can comment on it over and over again
sign divorce papers with your lucky pen
hopefully you'll never have to work again
I'm not the only one who's not decisive
even as I write this I'm in crisis
a gaping hole between free and priceless
I don't really like this life it's too lifeless

this life is too lifeless

And he prescribed me
a time machine
was at the doctor's as part of my dream
And he prescribed me
a time machine
with a magic watch on his wrist with a laserbeam

Barking Japanese to the moon and the stars
thinking bout space travel and those new flying cars
seems so real in a trip,
you see the sea from the cliff
talking about the future
your dormant frozen stiff

don't look down on me
I won't look down on you
there is no height or economics to do
in my mind, can't rewind, travel back in time

The hours fly by, the days drag in
The doctor's diagnosis couldn't fix him
up in smoke, the door, back to before
Remote control brain what do clocks tick for?

I got woken up by a phone call to say one of my best friends had died. I was still half-sleeping on the couch and had a moment where I struggled to comprehend what was reality. I remember a vivid image of a doctor shooting laser beams out of his wrist which at the time seemed more real than the phone call I had received. I would later head to the library to check my Bebo, hoping I had imagined the news, but before that I wrote most of the words that would later become Time Machine Prescription. *I think out of all the early songs this one still stands the test of time and I really wanted to sample it for* Dreams Are Mental. *It may not appear on the new album in any physical form but it definitely would go on to inspire the later work.*

JEREMY KYLE

Dear Deidre my wife is a slut
She stole all my money and now I'm depressed
Jeremy Kyle made her confess
After she failed the pregnancy test

Dear Trisha my life is a mess
Dear Deidre printed my full name and address
What did my friends do?
They just took the piss
They don't realize how serious all this is

Tell me what to think,
Tell me what to do
Cause I'm a nobody compared to someone like you
Tell me what to do, what to do with my life
Because Jeremy Kyle has been fucking my wife

Dear Montel, my life's a living hell
After your show I've been taking it well
It was all going swell if I truly confess
Going well until my wife flashed her breast
Now the whole world can see her right boob
I know you censored it but not on YouTube

Tell me what to think,
Tell me what to do
'cause I'm a nobody compared to someone like you
Tell me what to do what to do with my life
Because Jeremy Kyle has been fucking my wife

Although I am trying to avoid specifically defining any of these lyrics, I feel like I should partly explain this one as it was definitely very misunderstood. It breaks my heart when someone says "I like yer song 'Jeremy Kyle has been shagging yer wife'" or similar. Missing the full point. It started with a bass riff from Martyn Yuen as we both jammed at Dixon Street Studios. I didn't have any lyrics on me so looked around the room for inspiration to see a Dear Deidre letters page that was a mainstay of The S*n *newspaper. I started playing around with the idea of sending her a letter. Before social media, we had newspapers, magazines, soaps and chat shows that would make money off mocking the poor and also specialised in exploiting the insecurity of seeking perfection. This has obviously sky-rocketed since we now have targeted ads on social media and Photoshop, filters and now AI creeping into our daily lives. I noticed that certain people I knew would seem happy until they picked up a magazine or watched one of these shows. It was fucking with people's heads and in the story of this song, my wife's specifically. I have never ben married. It's not a true story. The album version also mentions John Major and John Terry who had scandals at the time and seemed fair game. Jeremy Kyle was and is still fair game as he was one of the most reprehensible human beings ever to darken a television screen. Jeremy Kyle fucked my wife had shock value but it also had a double meaning that isn't initially very obvious. It became our biggest 'hit' of that era, getting around 40k views for a rubbish YouTube video I filmed and edited at the Soundhaus, and to my surprise one day I got an email from Paul Heaton of* The Beautiful South *and* The Housemartins. *He said he wanted to play the song on BBC 6 Music and needed a radio edit. I thought it was a wind-up but replied with an email saying something like "I don't know how to make a radio edit" and then, on my birthday, the song was actually played on the radio. A 6* Music *producer had reversed all the swear words and let the song air. Depsite the censorship it was still completely obvious what the words were. Shout out to Paul Heaton: with his backing we ended up with fans and friends in Salford, and his co-sign opened the door for other DJs and bloggers to start treating us a wee bit more seriously.*

'the Girobabies tell it like it is, like it was, and more importantly the way it's going to be. Long live the Girobabies!'

Paul Heaton

LIQUID SKY

It was a liquid sky a noise distorted
An invisible man whose ashes were snorted
Birds were crawling as insects floated
The cave was empty mountain sugar-coated
Landscape still but still remind me
Of the day I prayed nobody would find me
Happily depressed this has been destined
Failed success deliberately mentioned
And as I swim upon the hillside
I laugh and I cry and I think 'When will I...
Make it back to the place I chose to leave'
Those lies in my head that I chose to believe
Return to that hell I dream of daily
Heavenly peace is a lot more scary
There is no ecstasy in safety
If I fail nobody claims they made me
All I wanted was some peace and quiet
Now all I want is a full-scale riot
The daily doses of mental strain
Kept my mind away from the glaringly obvious
Now the lie low is my crown of thorns
Boredom and fear is what I rely on
A flash and a crash of thoughts repeated
Being the winner who stands defeated
Independent rush of the blood was non-productive
Non-conductive energies are always so assumptive
A moonsault from an astronaut
Over a planet that's long forgot
That's been and gone
What's that? What's what?
You were earning a little but were learning a lot

How high liquid sky
How old before you die
How low before you try
Who? What? How? Why?

I must have been very high when I wrote this. I remember listening to it back for the first time on an MP3 player walking through an Ayrshire scheme at night and loved the grand finale. It was more close to the more experimental music that I was listening to, that I wanted to make. It never made the final cut of the project but was online for a while and was a bonus track on the re-release. I remember Hazy's guitar solo and all the weird effects making me feel happy and sad at the same time. I was going through a lot at this point and I remember it vividly making me want to keep going. Shout outs to Martyn on backing vocals and bass. It was him who got me and Hazy into a studio and found our first drummer, Claude from Marseille. Without his enthusiasm and support then I doubt we would have even got this far.

PARTY AROUND ME

party around me
and I'm fucking glad peer pressure found me
do me a favour
pray to yer saviour and see if you can stop my
    anti-social behaviour

it's called being constructively disruptive
independent rush of the blood was non-productive

party around me
and I'm fucking glad peer pressure found me
do me a favour
pray to yer saviour and see if you can stop
    my anti-social behaviour

This was a bonus track and had a few different versions over the years. Originally I made a version with an electronic beat with Pete Mullen which also featured Katya Miakish on the piano. It was very spacious, repetitive and simple. I loved it but felt like something was missing so we tried in vain a few different versions. One included a rap verse that I did that Robbie and Gordy would forever refer to as 'my first rap song', which is about 32 bars that I have memorised so well that I can bring out of retirement no matter how worse for wear I am. I won't bore you with the lyrics here but if you ever see me doing an impromptu verse over some techno, DnB or a jazz band then there is a good chance you will hear me start the process with 'they call me outgoing cause I am always going out...'. When we later re-released Social Not Working + Bus Stop Apocalypse *together as one CD we included the* Clinker *remix as a bonus version. Pete and Tomoko of* Clinker *were one of the first people to show a keen interest in what I was doing, and they have regularly remixed us and even once hosted us in that London during our first tour.*

A collection of words that were roughly put together between 2008-2010. We had earlier works but I consider this the definitive debut release. We were young and had no idea what we were doing. The themes were described as 'baffling ned punk' by The Evening Times. *I have no idea if it was meant as a compliment or an insult but we ran with it as it has always been quite hard to pigeonhole anything that we have done. We also got compared to* The Fall *and Alex Harvey. Two acts that I didn't know much about until people said we reminded them of them but naturally became a fan after the fact. Artwork by Jerry Dowds shows Glasgow crane workers going on strike and spelling out 'YA WANK' as a message to their bosses. We were unemployed and going to the social to sign on back then just as the phrase 'social networking' was starting to gather pace. The project was released at The Buff Club as part of an* Old Jock Radio *night. The album was recorded, mixed and mastered in the hidden lane at Elba Studios, Glasgow by Stephen Scott.*

CHAPTER TWO:
BUS STOP APOCALYPSE

2012

WHAT VICTOR SAID

Boys will be boys if the monsters sell them toys
Annoyed by all the silence
Annoyed by all the noise

And he said
Hit him on the head
That's what Victor said
Hit him on the head with a baseball bat
Are you gonna take that?

There was a place near Central Station called Victor Morris. It was where musicians bought guitars and the young team bought weapons. Some did both. I think it was a pawn shop that found a grey area where they could sell swords and the like based on the fact they were 'antiques' or 'collectables' but I don't think that is a thing anymore. If the last album was a Hazy album then this is probably half Hazy / half Robbie musically. This is definitely one of the songs you can hear Robbie's stamp over. I used to love playing this song live as the instrumental crescendo kicked in. Nothing fancy, just two minutes of indie punk that captures a time and feeling of the city of Glasgow.

OVERHEARD IN THE WESTEND

Overheard in the Westend
It's hard to tell who's real and who's pretending
Overheard in the Westend

Overheard in the Westend
He claimed the guy from *Belle & Sebastian* was his best friend

'It's the wrong dynamic'

Byres Road is Too Commercial
We want retro like a dress rehearsal
Before the matinee, private booth
On-hand butler while we rip off *Muse*
I'll wear my V.I.P. badge with pride
I'll be a student all my life
Pay good money for very bad charlie
Charlie Sheen meets Nathan Barley

Overheard in the Westend
It's hard to tell who's real and who's pretending
Overheard in the Westend
He claimed the guy from *Snow Patrol* is his best friend
Said with pretension

Organic quails' eggs hand-delivered
Designer shades on in a middle of a blizzard
Give me an apple not too tart or sweet
It's not for me but for the dog you see
Look down on Partick like a Portaloo
Champagne, Chinos and a Port Salut
Daddy's money buys social barriers
Iceland shopping in Waitrose carriers

I was standing outside a pub on Great Western Road and overheard some students talking about a BP oil spillage which was all over the news at the time. I don't know if these events make the news anymore since half of the UK's beaches are now dumps for sewage companies but it was big news back then. One student said to the other with a knowing nod 'You can't fully comprehend an oil spillage until you witness it on a high-definition television set' and that was it. Overheard in the Westend *was born. We recorded it live very quickly at Berkely Studios where Stuart Higgins brought a mobile recording setup too and that ended up being the version that made the album. The phrase quickly became bigger than the band, with an offshoot Facebook page getting over 25,000 followers in a few months while our band was still only around 1,000 followers. We are catching that meme page up but still around 20k behind it. This song was also an entrance theme song for a tag team of ICW wrestlers called S.T.I. who played up to the crowd as posh bad guys. I heard it unexpectedly when I went to one of their events and I thought I recognised the intro but guessed it was a* Placebo *song.* Overheard in the Westend *also became a monthly night that I ran in Cafe Siempre and Inn Deep which featured live music, poetry and comedy. It took a life of its own and in hindsight, if you allow me to put on my tinfoil hat for a second, may have actually damaged our career by upsetting some of the local tastemakers and gatekeepers. It worked well as a spoken word poem and we played it live last year at Carlton Studios for a secret show. First time we played that with a full band in years and it felt great. Was great to see the audience still knew the words. Fun fact: some people believe Eminem stole the melody for one of his choruses.*

NIGHTMARE

I awoke from a nightmare and it suddenly dawned
I'd been scammed and been conned and been wrong all along
it was then that I knew that monsters were real
it's good to receive but it's better to steal
your fishmonger eyes tell that you sell fish

first time I met you I knew you were a nightmare
angry little nightmare
your face would make a soldier throw down his weapon
his advantage and fight fair

you are a nightmare
angry little nightmare
you are a nightmare

the pope screamed Jesus Christ but it wasn't in vain
he was comparing with the queen all the wars in their name
who's bad who's good
who's misunderstood
who's separate by the way they interpret a book
your fishmonger eyes tell that you sell fish

hi there nightmare you're a nightmare

Hazy is convinced this song is about him and who am I to argue with a lead guitarist? I am the type of guy to definitely argue with a lead guitarist and while there may be some truth in his suspicion, he's only half right. I remember recording this in Robbie's house as his production chops were gaining momentum and he added some cool noises over the top which by memory could have either been an FX pedal but pretty sure it was a synth. Hazy was not a nightmare on this day. I remember him doing a great job. He was a brilliant guitarist and a comedy genius but could be difficult at times and blessed with a self-awareness that makes him suspect this song is about him but it's not really. I remember enjoying playing it live but it rarely made the cut after a while. I could feel my writing was improving but my delivery was still off. It's a frustrating place to be when you can't replicate the voice in your head on a record. Anyway, I don't care what anyone says 'Fishmonger eyes tell that you selfish' is a great line and sorry I am willing to die on that hill.

COUNTDOWN TO TINNITUS

People talk about ONE self TWO much
at any given Second
in the THIRD person
go FORTH and drink a FIFTH of gin
Ive got a SIXTH sense for the SEVENTH deadly sin
I should've EIGHT something
before the NINE bar subcrawl
playing TENNIS with tinnitus
in a tunnel feeling awful

Clock ticking on my ear's innocence
bus stop apocalypse
countdown to tinnitus

Five
Four
Three
Two
One

I broke through the TEN commandments
Like a cat with NINE lives
I lost my head like all of Henry the EIGHTH's wives
I slept through the SEVENTIES
awoke the SIXTH of June with a sick sense of humour
Let's bet our landlords FIVE hundred monthly rent based
purely on a taxi-driver rumour
I ate FOUR bidden fruit with the THREE wise men

Went TWO church in fancy dress ONCE never again
The silence keeps me awake at night
it's the feedback
the white noise
the wind chimes
it goes through me

I remember being really excited when we dropped this as a single. It felt fresh at the time and a good indication of where we were as a band. Hazy writing great riffs, Robbie adding textures and samples, and Lu Angel adding guest vocals. We were a 6 or a 7 piece at this time. Martyn and Claude had left to travel the world so we were bringing in a variety of bass guitarists and drummers plus we were now regularly adding synths and backing vocalists alongside two and occasionally three guitarists. We weren't quite there yet but it was unpredictable and fun. Haven't even heard this song in so long never mind play it, but I regularly do it as an acapella and ask the crowd to count to ten and raise my hand every time they need to say a new number. It's a good way to get the audience to shut up and interact especially during an acoustic or spoken word set.

IDIOT'S GUIDE TO KARMA

I was young, stupid and broke
needed something to read
put it in my rucksack cause it wasn't cheap cheap cheap
I was on my way out
then the buzzer went beep beep beep
brass neck
onlookers chuckled
in the store detective's grip
I was huckled
they ignored my pleas of please don't phone the police
then had a read
it was the stupidest theft that they'd ever heard of

> I just shoplifted the idiot's guide to karma
> they had to let me know they didn't want any drama

The police wouldn't jail me
or even took the book
they just shrugged their shoulders and shot me a look
worried that the bad vibes would rub off on them
and from theirs to theirs
and his to hers and theirs to there's
I didn't understand
till I read it on the train
then the penny dropped on my one-pound brain
I couldn't give it away, I couldn't give it away

Oh, I wanna wake up in Tokyo
somewhere the book would never know
burning pages makes no difference

burning pages can't ease no conscience
I couldn't give it away, couldn't give it away
the karma
they had to let me go they didn't want any drama

using earplugs on the train
blocking out the chaos
I need not a curer
just silence from these voices
today they speak in glowing terms about everyone
in fact as long as they all shut up
there'll be no need for that rock what's in my rucksack
buried deep
from my deep sub-conscience and my childhood
although now we barely speak speak speak speak

I remember waking up one day with an overwhelming feeling of wanting to be in Tokyo. It was probably a reflection on where I was at, both mentally and physically. I wanted to escape. This piece is about escape, consequences and shoplifting. Tokyo felt the most opposite place I could go at that time in my mind. It was our new bassist John McCrory who co-wrote the music on this one. He brought his bass to my flat and we just recorded the thing from start to finish. I never made it to Tokyo although I got reasonably close a few years later when I was The Twistettes' *roadie in South Korea.*

SHONZO THE SECURITY GUARD

no drugs no entry confiscating ever

no drugs
no entry
confiscating everything
later on he sells you it back

shonzo the security guard,
he'll let you fill your pockets coz he knows times are hard
shonzo the security guard,
moonlights as a bouncer, the man in charge.

This is a strange one. I was asked by my mate Shonzo to make a song for him. I think he gave us £100 so me and Robbie split the money and made this song in one night. Robbie did all the real work as I just wrote and recorded a few words to sing over the soundtrack. I loved the fact that it made the album. It really shouldn't have but I always wanted to surprise the listener every time they hit that play button. Shonzo was neither a bouncer nor a store detective but he had a high-vis top and wore it for the music video that was filmed on the last weekend of the Soundhaus. The greatest nightclub Scotland ever had in my opinion. I don't know where I would have been without that happy place. If you watch the video on YouTube you can see we played a prank on the crowd, and some of the band. I sparked a cigarette and Shonzo then proceeded to throw me and the rest of the band offstage as the sound engineer let the song play. I don't think the rest of the band knew what was happening. Shonzo just started chucking folk out. He didn't even work there. And, even if he did, Soundhaus was not the sort of place to throw a band offstage for smoking. And even if they were it was shutting the next day. That's why the crowd looks so confused. I love it on the rare occasion that a DJ plays this song in a club.

"the low-fi electronica influenced `Shonzo The Security Guard` is an unexpected Irvine Welsh acid trip, a frenzied affair packed full of rave witchery and dirty club basements"

mojophenia.com

I WANT ANSWERS

easily lead
like the fear you dread
the panic attack
when your eyes go red
the spanner in the works
if it works you must be gullible
to think it won't break
your gonna lose what you got
just admit and keep on walking
crawl up the stairs
pretend you're not talking
shocking state of affairs
we always end up
thinking up plans cause we're so damn fed up

> too many scapegoats, too many chancers
> I hope that I wake up and I'll finally get answers
> too many questions
> keep your suggestions
> I want answers

blood on your hands of greed
skates on your feet
you'll still smell of roses if you delegate deceit
don't listen to me, your friends or the news
for every wise word you'll hear a hundred thousand fools
there's a smile on my face
in my heart there's resentment
urban jungle of cement it's a peasant's contentment
let's never speak again but I'll call you tomorrow
say sorry with a threat yes, beg, steal, borrow

> too many scapegoats, too many chancers
> I hope that I wake up and I'll finally get answers
> too many questions
> keep your suggestions
> I want answers

It's a two horse race and we're running from the chase
with guilt and remorse and it's written on your face
stamp mug on your forehead
we were all born yesterday
we will all die tomorrow
every day is judgement day
Yay!

Robbie turned this from a middle-of-the-road indie song into something interesting with the synths and using coins in a bucket as percussion. I remember carrying these lyrics written on a scrap of paper for about a week or two before I had a chance to jam it out. But I can't listen to this song without immediately being thrown back to the time at the Edinburgh Fringe where we filmed this music video. Gordy was dressed in a bogging and evil-looking Tweety Pie outfit, and we had just played a disastrous show as warm up for our friend Becky. I had wrote a show on the bus over called The Psychoanalysis of Noel Edmonds and Andy Murray's Maw. *The show was terrible but the crowd didn't help us. When I got stuck or put my foot in it I invited a hesitant Robbie and Gordy onstage to do some acoustic tracks. We got drunk with the small amount of money we made and had a great night even though we got flung out of The Hive. I'll maybe keep that story for the real book if it ever happens. But it was sunny and we were having fun so invited Andrew Mackenzie to come along on Day 2 to film us mucking about and he ended up doing a great job of capturing the high before the low. I also remember buying a bottle of champagne off a guy that turned out to be empty. The bottle you see in the video is empty, we just didn't know until we stopped filming and decided to pour a glass. The bouncers kept the bottle. Sometimes I wonder where it ended up.*

DRIP EFFECT

The drip effect of darkness
the constant cold is taking its toll
five hours later yourre ten miles from home
you only went for a stroll

talking football with a taxi driver
his disposition
his disposition is as bleak as yours

alienate everyone whenever you can
take a sedative north of Edinburgh
does that sound like a plan?
I lost my braincells somewhere between the Sub Club
   and the Classic Grand
hand them in if you can
I lost my ticket and my band

like a stray cat running down the railway line
the felines (feelings) unpredictable
and the train is timed

the drip effect of madness
this broken road is paved with mould
a wolf in sheep's clothing, cunning and bold
it's got you controlled
you were rushed
like a bill
swanked through parliament
on stilts and roller-blades
handled with oven-gloves
shotgun to your head

We went to a recording studio around Kinning Park / Cessnock way. Just myself and Robbie. Created it from scratch and it was finished that same day. Robbie was with me all the way during my writing process which was an unusual thing to happen, but with him looking over my shoulder, he definitely informed some of the lyrics. I feel like he deserves credit for the word 'swanked' as I have never used that word before or since. The music video for this was a one-take recording of Gordy galloping through the fields of Audio Soup Festival.

THE GIROS

Do I wanna be a spaceman?
Do I Fuck!
We want warehouse parties and amphetamine hugs
They want us to take vitamins and learn new skills
We want Giro days and ecstasy pills
we want outdoor tripping on sunny days
and nobody gives a fuck what the government says
I can't stand being in the rain
waiting on a train
ground-hog dead repetition ripping at the brain
mundane environment
teenage retirement
studied for a year but didn't know what his higher meant
he spent three years on a sheet of paper
three years to get 20 years to pay for
still have to graft as hard as your neighbour
nervous breakdown on your lunch-hour
save the heart attack for later
he's got his degree and he's finished his major
it didn't mean fuck all he's still a minimum wager

> It's the Giros
> It's the Giros
> It's the highs, the lows, the Jies, the Rose

Do I want to pay my train fare?
Do I Fuck!
I'll just sit and read the paper and chance my luck
blatant train skipper
get off scot free from ScotRail
not a criminal but one time I got jailed
do I want to join the army?

Do I Fuck!
I'm not brave or fearless enough
to get blown up
in a war I don't believe in
the news is misleading
Rupert Murdoch cheerleading for the bible-reading

> Fuck the council tax bill
> I'll camp on a hill
> I'll camp on a hill
> I'll camp on a hill

get a job
get a job
get a job
get a real job
get a proper job
get another job
get a part-time job
with your full-time job
get a mortgage
get another one
get a hobby
not that one but another one

I suppose this is almost the theme song for the band. There have been so many highs and lows and this was one of the first songs we ever wrote, recorded and played live. Up until recently it was the last song at almost every show. You can tell how much the band is enjoying the night by how long it goes on with fake stops at the end. You can also gauge how much the audience is feeling the performance by how many people shout back 'Do I Fuck!' It appeared on The Broken Home Sessions *which was a CD we handed out over 300 of at* T in the Park *without any writing on the discs. So if you got one and enjoyed it then I apologise that you had no idea how to find us. The original was recorded in a flat in Ayr with Higgy but we re-recorded a version for the album that some people complained was 'too slick' (same thing happened with* Bank Charge *too as it goes because we took out the gang vocals) but yeah we really should have made a video for this song or something. It feels really weird listening to this back: I was very young when I wrote this but still enjoy performing it to this day. It does what it says on the tin. You will find as my writing progresses, I lose a lot of the simplicity but then after overthinking and overcomplicating everything. I did try to get back to that era for the new album but there is an energetic rage that only youth can capture sometimes.*

BIG SOCIETY

There's no stopping this apocalypse
If you say otherwise yer taking the piss
We're hoffing this shopping list
Out-of-date rolls with the ten pence crisps
Out of order, closed for business
Damage limitation so they shoot the witness
Cheap foreign labour and a lack of new ideas
Means a storms a'brewing and the rent is in arrears
It appears we're no longer pioneers
We'll be refugees in a matter of years
Looking for work, being shunned as one
Isn't it ornoc? The shutdown has begun

>   They shutdown society
>   Living underground
>   They shutdown society
>   Living underground
>   Living in a rundown industrial comedown

Who needs uni? Join the army!
Why be educated when you can be angry?
Global conglomerate the rise of the franchise
Shut down yer chip shop, monopolise yer French fries

It's a big, big society
Bin the idea of a career in psychiatry
Big, big society
Become a volunteer and sweep the floors of the library
Big society
Big society

Considering this was written in 2011 it's fairly prophetic from my younger self. Many people I know want to escape this island to have a better future. We have always been seeking refuge in sunny climates but we prefer the term ex-pat. How ignorant is that? It feels like we are being cut off from opportunities in Europe and anywhere else. The rest of the world is starting to shun us because all we do is create war and various other problems. The middle class is now starting to feel the same genre of rage that I felt all those years back. All we can do is hope for something to change soon but right now the racists want to leave the UK because there are too many immigrants and anyone who isn't racist wants to leave because they are sick of living under a right-wing government and media. I'm not saying everyone wants to leave this island but how many are truly happy? It's quite a miserable place to be right now and I expect the hateful rhetoric to multiply between now and the next election. I just hope the general public doesn't fall for immigrants being the fall guy (again) for austerity that our politicians and corporations cause. Anyway, the song has had a few different versions. We put the Pete Mullen mix as a bonus track on the re-release but it was a bit too long and felt like it was missing something. There is also a Sun Dogs *hip-hop mix that featured an all-star line up of Loki, Gasp, Mog, Physiks and Louie that was released on our secret album* Taxi Driver Rumour *(it was only available via taxi drivers that we handed the CD too and the first 50 people who ordered* Who Took Utopia? *on vinyl). There are also some good full-band live versions online that have a bit more of an edge, but yeah the song was basically abandoned after failure. Like people wanting to leave the UK. I*

FLUFFY PUPPY RAINBOW FLOWER

Not a cloud in the sky,
Not a tear in your eye,

Fluffy fluffy puppy rainbow flower

The sun is out and it's bright
Everything is alright
And it's a beautiful day
Everything is gonna be okay

This was in response to a reviewer who said I seemed to be incapable of writing a happy song. It was just happy guitars and happy words. The video features us dancing down a hill at Alexandra Park. It was later remixed by Flapsandwich of Sicknote *who turned it into a dirty bassy banger. It was originally just a joke song but people did like it so we added it as a bonus track on* Bus Stop Apocalypse.

This was mostly written and all recorded in the year 2012. We promised to drop an album by the end of the year and we did by the skin of our teeth with an album launch at a venue called Pivo Pivo on Waterloo Street on December 31st. The set went past the bells so we were trying to win album of the year for 2012 and 2013. We won nothing obviously. And still haven't. I was the in-house booker so we played a show there, then all went to the Soundhaus for an after-party. This album was recorded in various places by various people but Robbie Gunn did most of that side of things. Hazy wrote about half of the music and Robbie the other half, with John McCrory also chipping in with one. The album is a bit all over the place but I think it was a natural progression of chaos, and while it can be hit and miss at times, I am very proud of how different it sounds from the previous record, but still keeping that same sound whatever that is. Oh yeah 'baffling ned punk' remember? We initially burnt our own CDs and made our own DIY covers. I would love for anyone to send me a pic if you happened to get one of those. It was then re-released on streaming platforms and came out as a double CD alongside Social Not Working *many years later.*

CHAPTER THREE:
WHO TOOK UTOPIA?

2015

We wrote this in the afternoon and performed it live later that night in a barn somewhere east of Edinburgh heading towards the Scottish borders. It was an equinox party to raise money for Audio Soup Festival. I highly suspect it may have cost them money to put it on but it was a great night with a fun line-up so we wanted to have something a bit more upbeat, positive and festival sounding for the occasion. It's fair to say this became our biggest 'hit' of sorts. It somehow connects with the audience on a sunny outdoor stage as much as it does in a pub on a winter's night. No idea how these things happen or I would probably do it again. It is also our most streamed song ever and has our highest YouTube views. Every time a new song is about to catch up then Equinox *comes round twice a year and it runs off into the lead again. It also works as a spoken word poem too and works well for acoustic campfire jams. I think full credit has to go to Robbie Gunn on guitar and production plus Green Door on mastering. It's as close to a pop song as we have / will ever make. And it opened doors for us to play many festivals including the main stage of Equinox Festival on Chalk Farm near Grimsby.*

EQUINOX

Acting normal is a portable portal I report to
whether or not I'd even want to
I'm gonna fool you
Dear sunshine been a while since we last talked
round about the time the landlord changed my flat lock
glad that you're back lots
padlocked mad thoughts
since we flipped down the laptop and shouted TAPS OFF
SORRY CAPS LOCK ON and I meant to say taps aff
call a plumber this summer we're having the last laugh

So we shall see what we shall see
looks like we made it
looks like we made it to equinox

Acting normal is a portable portal I report to
whether or not I'd even want to
I'm gonna fool you
that late February sun,
zombies congregate and wobble under it stunned,
in many ways more potent than that late-June sun,
less drinking fines and definitely less sunburn,
the Seasonal Affective Disorder gets distracted,
the January Blues have been sung and lambasted,
the mad March hare has hibernated and fasted,
a spring in our step as winter's outlasted,
the best is yet to come and now we're past the bad bit

SECRET ANIMAL

    am not an arsehole
    am a secret animal
    it's been like this for a year or so

perched up high observing the madness
build a nest and blow it up and laugh at all the sadness
had this condition since the day time failed me
grew broken wings internal cranium duck beak
I walk with what used to be feet
you hear a grunt and a muffle as I shuffle down the street
molly-coddled ancient sheep, goat head, lost it
meddling penguin peddled nonsense 'till they bought shit
a slug is a snail with no house... unlike turtles
the voice of a tortoise as he fatally hurtles (!!!!)
the hurdles overcame
the tigers broke the rules
played chess with all the monkeys and blagged them like fools

    am not an arsehole
    am a secret animal
    it's been like this for a year or so

Secret Animal *was the first single to be released off the album and was played on* BBC 6 Music *by one of my all-time inspirations Steve Mason of* The Beta Band *and he invited us to support him at Liquid Rooms in Edinburgh. I remember the pure fear of being stuck in traffic and having to grab a last-minute backline for our set because something predictable and well within our control had happened earlier in the day. It all went well in the end. It was also then played by Tom Robinson on 6 Music but led to complaints due to the language. I never asked them to play it so there wasn't a radio edit. There is a minor 'shit' but it's said too fast in a Scottish accent so I reckon that fell under the radar and it was more the blatant 'arsehole' that is shouted repeatedly fairly slowly. The few radio plays that have followed have always asked us directly if we can confirm if there is swearing or not plus a full copy and paste of the lyrics within the song. I think they got bored of that and now we haven't had any radio plays on the most recent album despite it not having any swear words at all. This was also the first time I attempted 'the birthday single' by releasing a song on my birthday to take advantage of social media traffic. 'Thanks for all the birthday messages, check out my new single etc.' It's a sadly overused and irritating tactic these days and you can maybe blame us for starting the trend. I don't mind people stealing my ideas. I have too many ideas to complete to fruition if I lived to a thousand. I also have a strong suspicion we might have stole this song from Elvis who would have stole it from a higher-skilled and sadly overlooked Blues musician.*

MIRRORSHOW

I just wanted to show you I miss you and hold up a mirror
and let you see the legend we all see
already did my to-do list today
coz it's more of a list of the things I did already

I've accomplished breakfast and it's not even lunchtime yet
we're here for a good time not for a long time

I just wanted to show I can change show you I'm not strange
baked you a cake with my name on it
I fell asleep and I dreamt you seduced me
now I'm awake you tell me that meant nothing

This song was used by Sky Sports on Goals of the Week. *I have no idea why. We never pushed it at all, never made a video and rarely played it live because it never really made the cut after we learned the rest of this album properly. I can only assume Steve Mason might have recommended it as we was on the Soccer A.M around the same time. I suppose it's quite nice and fairly television friendly. Neither Sky nor PRS ever coughed up for that one. PRS owe us about 15 years' of live music royalties. They have stressed me out and caused me too much anxiety by putting me through a Kafkaesque bureaucratic nightmare after deleting all my details then asking me to email and then an email asking me to phone then a phone call asking me to email. You get the idea. It stressed me out so much that I gave up but every day I get stronger and one day I will return.*

BRAIN ROCKET
(AND THE EVOLUTION OF TURTLES)

It's not rocket science all merits are dubious,
a flash in the pan from the dead-pan curious,
bravado steeped in irony,
steamed up windows (car-keys in the bowl)
zip it shut! close it up! kick down the door!
and glue together a little ship,
demolish each boat brick by brick,
Hollywood agents, cosmetic surgeons,
(give them all a nobel prize)
jabs and shots and GM crops it's
(no surprise these people ain't wise)
camaraderie showboat fisherman,
senses weakness 'n' sticks the boot in,
delicate flower—draped in poison,
she steals a glance then—reels the boys in,
I'd admire and hire the architect,
who burned his blueprint to light his cigarette

by the book structures—void and ludicrous,
it's not rocket science all merits are dubious,
full ay this,
ludicrous,
who is this?
the turtle is 150 years old
the turtle is 150 years old
the turtle is 150 years old
how do they know?

I remember it was really difficult to come with a name for this one. It was The Turtle Song *then* Brain Scientist *then* Rocket Surgery *but it needed more turtle. Pretty shite name we ended up with to be honest and everyone still calls it* The Turtle Song *anyway. This was sculptured in a kitchen at a house party and sometimes it still lives there. I think this one has proven to me that the human psyche while limitedly complex can usually enjoy a wee sing-song about elderly turtles and the systematic whitewashing of historical facts. There is a line or two in this one that even Robbie told me he liked. It is also the only song where we made that wanky hispter move all the cool bands do of changing instruments. Was always good to see bass maestro John McCrory getting behind the drums and Gordy joining the front line on guitar and backing vocals. Gordy refuses to sing backing vocals as a drummer despite clearly being the best singer in the band. 'Ye either want me tae drum or ye dinnae. If am drumming then but am no singing like Phil Collins or something.'*

LATE NIGHT SKETCHY

Don't be scared of me I'll be you when you wake up
I am not a hobby you can suddenly shake off
tried to get off the grid but the grid got gridlocked
off the radar by a campfire she charmed the smoke off
I smelt petrol then I saw a spark and she said
'you need to go now' anywhere but anywhere
a heroic dose of wine arrived via astronomy
Achilles heel on wheels with an in-built apology
have a laugh after all I'm told I'm only half lonely
I barge through the graveyard they telled me staff only
sorry the dreams you were sold were not meant for your sort
the dreams you dreamt were only meant for the other ones
and if by magic it were late night sketchy hey hey
follow me we'll have a very, very nice time

I'm wondering now as I donder around
on the fringe of the gutter with my head in the cloud
I'm wondering now as I donder around
on the fringe of the gutter with my head in the cloud
the clock struck three and it were late night sketchy
time to operate the heavy machinery
as if by magic it were late night sketchy
don't you operate that heavy machinery

Full steam ahead I'll make it up to ye
blistering, slithering poisoned fuckery
the moon did roar as the blood flowed underfoot
whats the matter? We're all howling in the moonlight
and if by magic it were late night sketchy hey hey
don't you operate the heavy machinery

Andrew Wetherall played this on his radio show after a friend of mine gave him the vinyl in Paris.

I wrote this one staggering back from the city with toothache after performing in front of 20,000 people at George Square. It was just before the independence referendum. I was numbing the severe pain by sipping whisky and potentially painkillers. (DO NOT DO THIS.) I remember getting a shot of a friend's hotspot to use my phone. This was the first time I had saw this technological witchcraft. I remember that blowing me away outside the Wetherspoons that has since taken over the square, that's when it's not under yet another renovation. I remember there being hope in the air that day. I went onstage just after Janie Godley and did a few spoken-word pieces like Bank Charge, Big Society, *etc., and a few* Jackal Trades *numbers plus, for one night only,* Alistair Darling's Eyebrows of Mass Distraction *which went viral on an app that became TikTok. Last time that happened.*

Also one I wrote especially called Eve of Revolution. *I remember going for drinks then getting refused entry to a bar. The bouncer saying 'Mark, I know who you are. Just go home please' so I made the long walk back to Ibrox feeling sorry for myself with my tail between my legs. The lyrics were spoken into a voice-notes app on my phone and must have made a big enough impression at the time to write them when I got home which is not something that ever really happens. Voicenotes is where my words usually go to die. Interestingly, the line 'swirling whisky for the tooth decay, the highlight of my day,' and the rest of an unused verse was on that same page but wouldn't get used until this year when we released* This Not Circus *on the new album. It was quite fun to co-write with my younger self. On the album version, you can hear the pain in my voice. I was about to lose my voice. More on that later on* No Place like No Place *but first time listening back to the album version for years. It's also the first time you hear Jo D'arc on a* Giros *song as she was joining the band as the album was getting finished replacing McCrory on bass. This still gets played live to this very day but the live version is completely different as the song was too long to maintain that loungey jazz club vibe. This was a single that was launched with a party at McChuill's on High Street and spawned 30 remixes which are all available on Bandcamp. The live version is far more frantic and raucous but nice to hear it again as nature intended. Fun fact:* If By Magic *is the name of this book and is a lyric that appears in* Late Night Sketchy.

BRING POTIONS

the birds are meddling
the dust unsettling
test-tubes bubbling
babababubba back-peddling
bunsen burnering
hot seat leveraging
questioning Leveson
bring me everything
I don't have a crystal ball all I do is pay attention
I see round corners when I feel my medicine
throw a message in a bottle of gin and ease the tension
are you fending for yourself or defending a pretend thing?

bring me my potions

realizing the fear is rising
this bleak horizon
I'm not hiding
I'll fight on if we can keep the light on

black cat waddles in the puddle he's muddying
born in Dennistoun claims to be American
get Alexander Bell on the phone next to Thomas Edison
a Tesla lightbulb moment switch it up to factor Ten
rip it up, start again, bring me my lucky pen
the man in the lab-coat wants to have that chat again
am adamant that mannequin wants to get the craic again
mad at the god-damn lack of any Anadin

realizing the fear is rising
this bleak horizon
I'm not hiding
I'll fight on if we can keep the light on

not in my name, not in my nature

they don't have nicknames no more
they only have bar-codes
then they rally cars of yours
around those bad back roads

babababa bring me my medicine
babababa bring me my everything

The phrase was coined during a conversation with Gordy who was my flatmate at this time in reference to another flatmate. He had left Perthshire to become our full-time drummer after we bumped into each other at Stereo and he reminded me he had drummed for us once at Twa Tams when our drummer had went AWOL. After filling in *boom boom* for a couple of shows he moved to the city somewhere between Bus Stop Apocalypse *and the start of recording this one. I remember the whole band recorded this in a big fancy studio meanwhile I recorded my bit in a flat using a microphone with some tights wrapped around it to stop the popping. I also remember Robbie telling me not to use the 'questioning Leveson' line as it was too topical. I think he was right.* Louder than War *called* Bring Potions *'a bunch of psycobabble but I quite enjoyed it' before giving the album a 9/10. Jo really adds a lot to the vocal performance and Robbie did a great job on the synth.*

PLANET FORT KNOX

to my credit I was drinking slowly
and to my detriment... I wasn't really
it's all swings and roundabouts
hocus pocus smoke and mirrors
post-man on high-alert whenever he delivers
and if I ever look confused?
Don't worry mate I'm getting ya
just correlating data dat may one day unsettle ya
people want the truth but don't care for facts
they want a black 'n' white soundbite as a green light to react

I'm not angry
to say I was suggests am somehow surprised
and I'm not shocked
not one jot
it's all so very predicable
also very avoidable
crowbarred mental block mind-warped brainwashed bubble
I have my own theories—I'm the king of this rubble

my wall is a towering inferno
until I bash in a keypad with my pin-code
motion captured lasers for good measure
vandal grease? nah! retina sensors
full of beans... in the bunker for the Alex Jones end time
refined tonic wines and a beware of the dug sign
I patrol my yard solo in a tin-foil jeep
and vet the wildlife for bugs cuz slugs can be discreet

I'm not lonely
better to have not loved than be lost forever
and I'm not bitter not one bit

ah researched the text of all the ancient scrolls
visitors not welcome round here no more
no time for fools I've disowned them all
down the shutters go forever I'm invisible

intruders get electrocuted trespassers prosecuted
by my law, my land, my rules, my gun
I shoot onsite with a remote control (bang)
my fence is spiked with barbed wire for defence
get out my head this is my patch
get off my land keep off the grass
move along there's nothing for you here to see
planet fort knox with a paltry population of just me

I'm not crazy
to say that I am says more about you
and I'm not wasted
I just say shit
I'll stay on the real while you live your cartoon
a glutton for punishment judgement day soon
my rifle and my bible just me and the moon
I'd rather that than blindly consume
sheep follow sheep ba ba to the abattoir
gabbing blah blah from your armour of an avatar
sheep follow sheep ba ba to the abattoir
gabbing blah blah from your armour of an avatar

intruders get electrocuted trespassers prosecuted
by my law, my land, my rules, my gun
I shoot onsite with a remote control (bang)
my fence is spiked with barbed wire for defence
get out my head this is my patch
get off my land keep off the grass
move along there's nothing for you here to see
planet fort knox with a paltry population of just me

An ode to my younger self who smoked too much hash and watched a lot of YouTube documentaries. We released it the week before our album launch at Stereo with a video that the brilliant Martin Windebank pulled out of thin air. I was the only person who turned up to the shoot and all we had was a camera and a psychedelic lab-coat then we made a tin foil face mask in my kitchen. I have no idea how Martin made something so interesting visually, so quickly, with so little. I also remember changing the opening line at the very last minute before I recorded the take. Can't remember what the opening line used to be but I remember it being pish. The promo got very weird as we followed the patterns and connected the dots after Yorkshire Tea, allegedly, stole our album cover idea with a billboard outside my house saying BREWTOPIA. This took us to Sunny Govan radio where we were interviewed by David Blackburn who used to work in marketing for Yorkshire Tea. Weirdly enough, Yorkshire Tea then started sponsoring The Libertines *or something and people thought it had been a well-thought out marketing ploy and were getting funded by the tea people. The conspiracy theories backfired on us. We were never paid by any hot beverage company ever. Or were we?*

NO PLACE LIKE NO PLACE

who took that?
who said what?
looking up to a scapegoat downing their luck
it's not my
it's not my fault
burnt at the stake but were promised rainbows
the emperor reigns but we're still wearing the same clothes
there's no new we

picture the scene a man out of his depth
they said that they would call nobody called me yet
are you there?
the raindrops drip and seem to rip the concrete
peaked too soon and now we're creeping off-piste
home!
oh!

what you say and what you do
one of the Two remains exhumed by the few
some rules
don't apply
indoctrinated quicker with a contradictator
the contraband banned by a cowboy crusader
there's no new
there's no new me

picture the scene a book out of its shelf
just a cobweb that malicious spider left
can you spin?
the hailstones hailed down a taxi driver
rumours started over jars over cider
home!
there is no place like it
oh!
maybe there is no ...

This is quite emotional to listen back to for many reasons but you can make up your own mind about that stuff. Most Girobabies *songs up to this point are recorded in a couple of takes but this took all day. I was just back from Knockengorroch Festival and my voice was completely gone. We thought at the time I had just overdid it but it would later become obvious that I was losing my voice when I was behaving and looking after myself, my voice would vanish. It turned out to be a large vocal polyp and would put the band on hiatus for a while. Luckily, the operation turned out okay in the end but it was a terrifying time. I wasn't allowed to speak for weeks and for anyone who knows me that was a challenge. I still kept my 'never cancelled, never will' policy up by playing Drygate in Dennistoun using a robotic voice on a phone app and did my usual spoken word set, joined a hip-hop cypher sand-covered* Fitter Happier *by Radiohead. FUN FACT: Utopia translates in ancient greek as 'No Place' hence the title.*

RAMP UP THE THEATRE

a swarm of shopping trolleys these knights will fly by
to your left is a seagull to your right is a high-rise
the closest thing to human life is a condom on the beach
and a ramp up the theatre

the bar lies empty and the landlord's ragin
the waste ground's rampant and the factory's vacant
the bus route is roulette pogo-hopping on a landmine
and a ramp up the theatre

the swing-park's shutdown an abandoned warehouse
and coming up ahead is where the old mayor camps out
the good buy goodbyes and sell their hellos in the meadows
and a ramp up the theatre

aaaaaaaaaaaaaaaaaaaaaaaaaaaaaaaaaaah!
yee-ha!
a way out!

I wrote this on a bus leaving Kelburn Garden Party on my way to a house in Irvine. Tom from Mungo's HiFi *asked to remix it as it reminded him of a clear up after an empty festival. I have no idea how he spookily sussed out that is exactly where I was based on these lyrics. I thought I was just writing a love poem to Ayrshire. We played this live on STV after repeatedly assuring the production team we wouldn't swear. The sound guy was randomly a guy called Mark who was our tour manger / driver / sound engineer during a fairly unsuccessful tour of England. It wasn't great. Leeds was especially bad supporting* Sicknote *(they were brilliant but the venue was not set up for bands and various other issues.) Thankfully the last show on the way home was at Knocky which in hindsight probably saved the band from completely imploding. I was just back from holiday but looked white as a sheet on TV. I think I drank too much free coffee in the green room or something. We also had to change our bassist at the last minute as John couldn't make it. Colin stepped in and learned three songs that afternoon before we went live. I was really, really nervous that day. We played three songs and I was interviewed but only ever watched back* Ramp up the Theatre *as that seems to be the only evidence of that day online. We stopped playing it live because the grand finale is too difficult to play with new band members coming in left, right and centre. FUN FACT: the phrase 'Ramp up the Theatre' doesn't mean what you think it does.*

ESCAPE! ROUTINE!

day 23 the truth is there is now daze now
the minutes seem minute compared to the months and hours
I row solo on this empty vessel
pacing up and down looking for a clue
or a footprint, validation, something
I don't know... anything
I think I see a monster of the sea
that local fork lore says is near to me
ha! fear is no match for this hunger eating up inside of me
yesterday, I made a fishing rod
out a bamboo shoot an a piece of string
and I launched my mythical dream catcher into the ocean
it made a thudding noise then vanished
there has been no 'man eating fish'
not on my watch
sun-clocks in the snow
the sand has long passed
and every so often I hear this buzzing noise that loops
that leaves me shook and propels me to jump through hoops
and stoop to new depths and look
can you hear that?

there's a helicopter overhead
escape! routine!
helicopter overhead
I know what's real

Dayeightyeight
things are getting silly now
a seagull serenaded me with a sea shanty
it whit?
I am what... !

must've been they zoo-keepers peaking through the cage
to protect us from ourselves and prepare us for the stage
the waiting game perpetuates the elusive magic flare
but I'm pleased!
I dream I can fly every night!
did you see that?
see that flash?

there's a helicopter overhead
escape! routine!
helicopter overhead
I know what's real

day 1 the snakes became butterflies
the pain became nothing but mere sleep in our weary eyes
it starts with a shooting star and parts with a sunrise
dazed by the beauty in everything—I felt good!
words are but a memory—I speak in colours now
I wanna spend another hunner summers with no count
fear was the temporary illusion of ego
we shed our last shred of sanity we don't need it now where we go
who took utopia?
well there's no place like the present
there's no passport for a state of mind
whether superstar or peasant
you took utopia!
and you are only me
and I was born yesterday so it was never really me
and aye I have sinned aye but it was never truly me
I quantum leaped into this instant and rose up from the sea
you have been trapped but you can break free
coz I think I spy a torch-light that will never bother me

We all take the same way out

We played this song for a few years before we recorded it. I used to pretend to have found a notebook and was reading someone else's poetry from it but I was actually freestyling different ideas that came to me onstage. Trying to find things that clicked and made sense in a surreal way. I also wanted to make it not rhyme whatsoever. I think it was actually Robbie's idea to do that. It's much harder for my brain to write and not make it rhyme as you can probably tell by reading these notes. FUN FACT: my vocal is too low in the mix. Robbie has admitted this even though it was his call. I didn't fight for more vocal as I was tired and wanted to just release the album. Both launch nights at Stereo and Barrowland Ballroom were probably our finest hours before everything would turn to shit again, for a while.

This was a massive leap forward for us as a band. It took longer than I would have liked but the results speak for themselves. By this point Hazy had left and Robbie Gunn took the lead on the music side of things. His writing, performances and production throughout are incredible. At this point we had no synth player in the band. Gordy and McCrory play all the bass and drums. We were a tight-knit 4-piece but Robbie started layering interesting textures that would demand regular keys players who joined after the album was finished. Jo D'arc joined mid-way through recording and added some iconic vocals in certain places and would play bass on tour as John left of his own accord suddenly. It was also mastered by Green Door studios in Govan who did an exceptional job. The last two records showed promise but were let down by inexperience, constant changing of the guard and a general shambolic approach to everything. I think whether you like this record or not you cannot deny that it sounds like a real band. WhO TOOk UtOpia? *has four circles to represent the four seasons and was the first time that as a writer I could actually link themes and stories together. There is another interesting thing about what four zeroes could represent but that's for another time.*

I just listened to it back there and it's actually not bad. Artwork by original bassist Martyn Nuey who by this point was an international jetsetter but would still help with graphics stuff and still one of the first people I ever send a new demo or idea to.

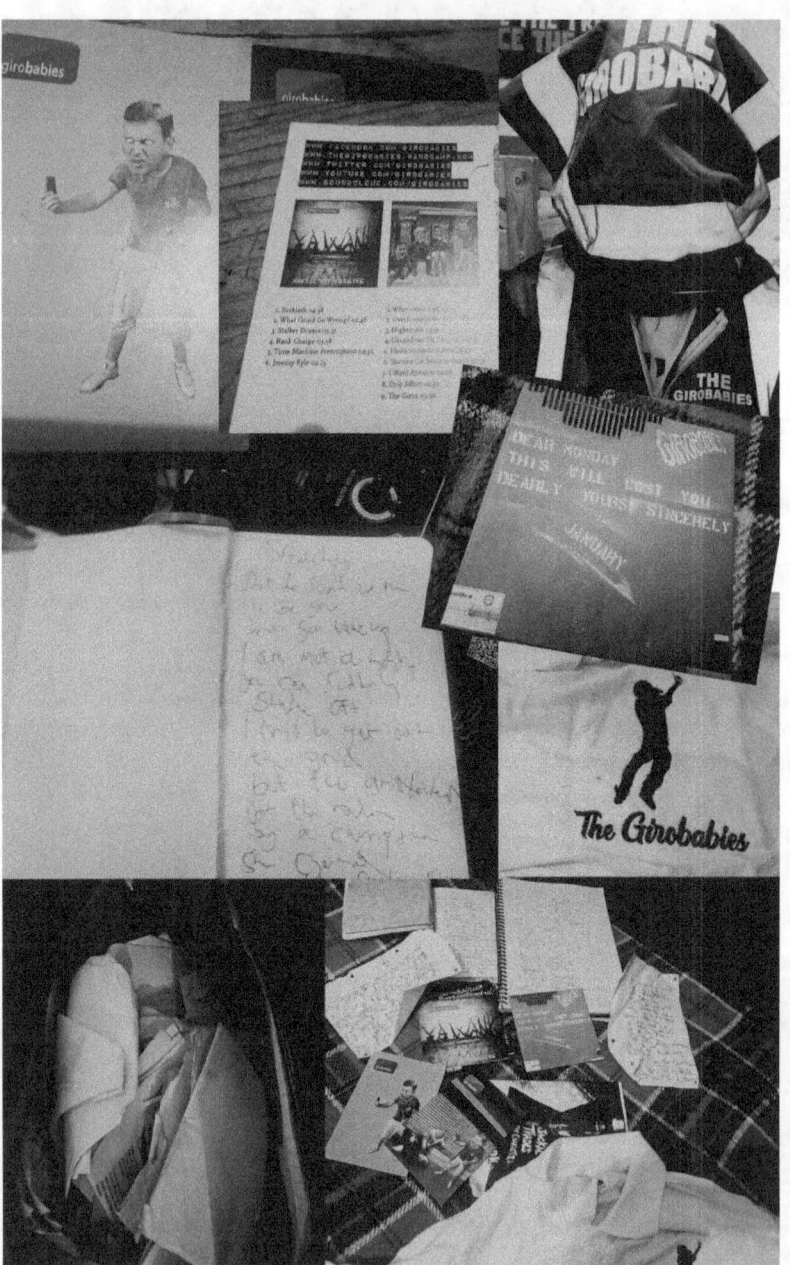

SHORT INTERLUDE

In between Who Took Utopia? *and* Dreams Are Mental *many, many years passed. I had throat surgery and when I returned we only played one more show with the old line up which was a Christmas gig at Stereo. I felt like life was too short to say no to certain shows and sadly neither Robbie or Gordy could commit. So we toured with new band members and recorded demos until I figured it all out. I released a few albums under* Jackal Trades *and a couple of attempts at a follow up* Giros *album were scrapped without seeing the light of day. Then lockdown happened and time just ran away from us all. We had a couple of singles namely* Dear Monday *and* Fetching Pitchfork *that are worth mentioning but if I include them in the book then I need to include the B-sides. If I include B-sides then I have to include the entire secret album T*axi Driver Rumour *and then there is all sorts of work that was released or remains unreleased and to save myself and publisher / editor Lucy a logistical headache we are going to move onto the final album Dreams Are Mental.*

I was determined / stubborn / naïve enough to finally make a follow up album but it took a while to find the right band members and also the right producer and place to record. I couldn't quit, and when it clicked, it happened quick, because dreams are mental.

CHAPTER FOUR:
DREAMS ARE MENTAL

2025

WE NEED AN INTRO

I didn't write any words for this one but I knew we needed an intro so I sent a voice memo to a few keys players to see if they could recreate the first song I remember ever writing. I must have been about 13 / 14 when I 'wrote' this. The words were rubbish but I was haunted by the tune and thought it would be good to include it in what is probably our last ever album. I tried to write to it recently but it was never good enough. Thankfully, Hal (with various aliases that includes Howdo Bean, Hal Dew, Howl Tiger, DJ Qwackerz) took my childish, monotone hum and turned it into an epic piece of piano music which was the canvas we used to set the scene for Dreams Are Mental. *I sampled a dream psychologist called Ian Wallace who gives a scientific definition of what dreams are. An old college friend, Stefan, introduced me to his work when he heard the album name and then about halfway through the track we switch to my friend Alan Gray who explains his own definition of what a dream is in his own inimitable style. The lush, imaginative keys of Hal combined with some additional samples from Morphamish bring it all together nicely and makes for a perfect post-punk wanky intro. I am aware that these sort of things are frowned upon but I know it's gonna start off punky and then get weird so this is a heads up to fans of weird music that it's gonna get weird and not just be 10 songs of me shouting. I want to start slow and strange so we can start properly.*

LANDFILL CULTURE

> The toon is deid, this city is deid
> Mid-range, mid week, am raging
> The toon is deid, this city is deid
> Have rage this week, am raging

More Polis than punters, where are the revellers?
There's a bam at central (muntered) repeating a mantra
He's murmuring something but I struggle with mumbling
But as I tumble closer his words are engulfing me (he says)

The toon is deid, why do we bother?
This city is deid why do we suffer?
This is not my first rodeo no this is my second
I've been here before and our surroundings have lessened
This place is getting worse
Does this city have a curse?
Dropped my wallet and her purse and I'm raging

I've done my time, I have earned my stripes
But I don't want to die in no countryside
I have micro-dosed, I have maxi-dosed
I awoke up on the Gorbals comatosed
Aw! so close! but just hit the post
There's a smell of burnt toast
And he's feeling pretty, pretty, pretty, pretty post-punk
Labrador pissin up the lampost

> The toon is deid, this city is deid
> Mid-range, mid week, am raging
> The toon is deid, this city is deid
> With rage this week, am raging

And my battery's deid and the queue is long
And the price is up and I don't know anyone (my wage is down)
I am raging, raging, raging
I am raging, raging, this place is getting worse

I was living in Mexico for the winter when this was released as a single. This is the ONLY time a song has ever had loads of streams on Spotify. I don't know if it's because it's very short, or the fact people were curious because I was on the other side of the world, or because it's a reasonably accessible punk banger but it got 20,000 streams in a month which is a lot for us (never ever used bots by the way; our below-average streams are all legit). It nearly overtook Equinox *in the first few weeks but it never did because nothing ever does. The idea came to me when I was trying to run a very unofficial Kendrick Lamar afterparty in the city centre featuring Kaptin Barrett who was up from Wales. It was a Tuesday and the day after Halloween. So Glasgow was partied out from a Thursday, Friday, Saturday, Sunday AND Monday of fancy dress. I was out flyering trying to get people in and I convinced a few people to forget about the door tax and just say 'Mark said it would be OK', sadly there was a miscommunication with my friend on the door so she told people they had to pay. The result was angry people not going in and when I tried to flyer again I literally couldn't see anyone, anywhere apart from one man in a high-vis and driving a roadsweeper who saw me and said 'the toon's deid' and I said 'that would be a good song name, am gonna make that a song' and he looked at me knowingly as if I was full of shite.*

FUN FACT: 'where are the revellers?' is an inside joke and I wish I had said 'regulars' instead of revellers.

THE SECRET INFORMATION

Video killed the radio star
Spotify killed the album
Mobile killed the landline
Policy killed the unarmed man
Smartphones killed the desktop laptop
Superfast fibre home broadband killed the dial up
Cocaine killed the pin-drop moments
As the cost of living is killing live music
And the house price rises killed our retirement
As corporate greed kills the natural environment

Aye aye, I got the secret information

> See that haunted house up on the hill
> If those walls could speak the secrets would spill
> Life moving fast, can't live in the past
> Enjoy each minute as it if it's yer last

Aye aye I got the secret information

As long as everybody here is cool with everything?
Nobody's ever really cool with anything
These days

Ketamine killed the post-club afters
Austerity killed all our mothers and fathers
Phone apps killed the home cooked dinner
Photo-filters killed getting naturally thinner
Content killed the TV, adverts killed the content
I-Phone killed the aux-in, clickbait killed our braincells

See that haunted house up on the hill
If those walls could speak the secrets would spill
Life moving fast, can't live in the past
Enjoy each minute as it if it's yer last

Aye aye I got the secret information

As long as everybody here is cool with everything

Is everybody here just cool with everything?
Is everybody here really cool with everything?
So is everybody here just cool with everything?
Nobody's ever really cool with anything
Is everybody here really cool with everything?
Nobody's ever really cool with anything
Since everybody here is cool with everything
Nobody's ever really cool with anything
I think everybody here is cool with everything
Nobody's ever really cool with anything
So long as everybody here is cool with everything
Nobody's ever really cool with anything
Aquí nadie nunca está de acuerdo con nada
These days

[Spanish intro parts by Helea Gimeno (Seiren)]

Quí nadie nunca está de acuerdo con nada
Hermanos de mi raza
Hermanos de mi sangre
Luchemos unidos para que se acabe,
Esta dictadura que nos pisotea
Que nos calla y reprime a balazos
Que nos mata de hambre y de vergüenza
Los Girobabies nunca se cansan

Teeth sent me a text saying 'as long as everybody is cool with everything?' and I responded with 'nobody's ever really cool with anything' because at that point the whole band was once again teetering on the brink of destruction. There was a lot going on. I'll save that for the real book if I ever write one. Honestly, Fleetwood Mac *would gasp at some of this shit. But the good news is we accidentally had a new hook which we needed as a missing piece of the jigsaw because the rest of it seemed solid. Dougie from* Mickey 9s *suggested I make it a call and response which made it even better and it felt nice to steal his ideas for a change. Kidding on.*

Our call and response gang vocals were provided by all the band members of the day Teeth, Jo, Gordy plus cameos from honorary band members Martin Windebank and Thomas Adams with some additional vocals and keys added remotely by Mima Merrow but last, and by no means, least was Helea Gimeno from Mexico City who took this song into a new stratosphere by adding singing parts but also reciting a Mexican poem of revolution throughout the song.

I felt like it needed some Spanish to jazz up the intro and her band Seiren *had blown me away when we were over there. Since then Mima Merrow and Debbie Love have done a terrific job of replicating her part when we do it live. Also shout outs to Josephine Sillars for attempting to do it. The* Dreams Are Mental *tour has seen both Mima and Josephine take turns on different shows and occasionally (The Barras gig and the Corbyn gig) they both united. Josephine would be first to admit her skills are far more musical than language based.*

FUN FACT: Gordy played the drums on this one and he did return to appear from time to time throughout the album.

ORDINARY DAY (3.33AM)

It was an ordinary day
That's what murderers say
It's abnormal that you thought to mention everything was
    normal to me
Zoom-in on an eyeball as I laugh at the screen
Solved another case with my armchair degree
I'm too nocturnal somehow turned into an animal
One day, likely, night time

Voice like a foghorn and a burglar alarm
Screaming bloody murder
It was an ordinary day
That's whit aw of them say

I never sleep, but when I try to, crows cause a scene
When my pillow finally feels so comfortable to me
I guess even creatures of flight
Have traits and ways to keep their edge at bay
Only the shopkeeper knows my secret
They keep it between them and me
They respect my custom and accept me meandering
  through aisle 3

It's me! It's me! It's me! It's me! It's me!

Please let the young team know
I'm a friend no a foe
I just don't take this road home
Very much, any more
But I'm up again
Who we up against?
I might be thirty something

But can still jump a fence

Searching for clues and footprints in the dark
Seeking justice and closure until the vengeance starts
I must've blacked out but there was good in my heart
I slept well in masel but why's there blood on my hands?
I slept well in my cell why's there blood on my hands?
I slept well in masel but why's there blood on my hands?

It's me! It's me! It's me! It's me! It's me!

It was an ordinary day
That's what murderers say
It was a typical ordinary day
That's whit aw of them say

By now, you may have started to notice a theme but, on another note, if you ever watch true crime and see grainy footage of a suspect or a witness being questioned by the police, at one point they will be asked to 'let's go back to the start, how did your day begin?' and if the suspect replies with 'well it was a typical, ordinary day' that means they are guilty as fuck. Apart from once. Once the guy was innocent. I would say 99% chance of being guilty. Innocent people don't tend to talk about how everything was normal. They are usually in shock because they have witnessed something traumatic not talking about how the birds were singing and how everything was completely normal because nothing about their current situation is normal. I think this is basically a middle-aged vigilante anthem where you metaphorically end up becoming what you hate eventually. And Mima Merrow's vocal at the end kind of morphed it into a James Bond theme song. I used to get told I had a voice like a foghorn quite often. I even got my ears syringed when I was at school because they suspected I was having hearing issues. If it wasn't true then, it is true now. The countdown to tinnitus is well and truly over since the album launch, and strange intermission, you had to be there. I also wanted to mention the word 'murder' because it's a good old Scottish stereotype the way we pronounce that word which I assume is down to 80s/90s detective series Taggart. *There is also a running joke that we can't say 'purple burglar alarm' which is only half true. Anyway, I think the shopkeeper caused all the commotion in this song. I also think rhyming 'myself' with 'ma cell' is an example of Scots language done correctly as it's the same word in Glasgow.*

FUN FACT: the song is called Ordinary Day (3.33am) *and it lasts 4.44 minutes. Coincidence?*

HER FANCY MAN

He's sliding in her DMs
Carte blanche carpe diem
Body is a temple, streaming in a steam room
Doon the gym selling crypto-scams
He's her fancy man

Yoga teacher, yogurt weaver,
Bought an awesome water feature
Only smokes when he's in Amsterdam
That's her fancy man

He's on the guesty, always cooshty
Gluten-free gourmet Japenese sushi
Profit on his last flat was 99 grand
Does a podcast from an ice bath
Calls it fancy man

In a seance, in a sauna
Manifesting lots of aura
Stocks and shares and a plot of land
A man about town
That's her fancy man

On the prop, RT , ladder
A multi million dollar man
Na na na na na fancy man
Na na na na na fancy man
Na na na na na fancy man
Faaaaaaaaaaaaancy maaaaaaaaaaaaaaaaaaaan

This is only one of two songs on this album that has any recognisable visuals yet. So when I listen to it, I see the work of Martin Windebank and his brother James. Half was filmed in New York, half filmed at The Barras. It took a lot of effort from multiple people with high-quality equipment in different parts of the world yet I can upload a video of me walking by the sea, with my old phone, and then add some text and it gets five times the views. It is so annoying. Especially since the time I spent making daft videos for social media I could have easily filmed and edited decent videos for every song on this album. Is our attention span so bad that we can't even watch a three minute music video now? It's destroying art, and culture. Every song that has a good video is instantly more powerful, effective and memorable and if we aren't careful then we are going to lose that. If I had a budget I would go for the high-quality music videos over more views and less effort. The budget is the thing because I am not a fancy man but I have started drinking lattes and even enjoy a cheeseboard at Christmas. The amount of lyrics I wrote for this was unreal. Jo advised me to scale it back and was correct and also suggested that there was no chorus until I had finished the scaled back version. I then decided to phone Calum and get a brass section in. I have jammed with the brass before but this is my first recording so thanks to Calum, Izzy and Colin for making it all a bit fancy. This is also one of the two songs that wasn't recorded at Sound Sound studios. It was recorded at Cumbernauld College. And what could be fancier than that?

FOGGY WINDOWS

    Smoke rises from the chimney
    Smoke rises from the chimney
    Smoke rises from the chimney

The flat lays abandoned with the ghost of flash points
Lingering around like insects to a house plant
Right digs shatters, left in tatters
The state of the estate agency for actors
A burnt-out gate adjacent to the welcome mat
A grave out the back AKA former cat
Foggy windows with finger prints on
That carve out initials but the temperatures wrong

    Smoke rises from the chimney
    Smoke rises from the chimney
    Smoke rises from the chimney

No postcode here, it's a trick question
The hounds of hell frothing and bleeding
Phone-in figments of imagination
Sold in segments, on eggshells, thin line of the needle
Blizzards gather hailstone face
Soaked to the skin such a maniac phase
The trees don't freeze cause they wear leaves as sleeves
And sneeze at the birds to get a buzz with the bees

    Smoke rises from the chimney
    Smoke rises from the chimney
    Smoke rises from the chimney

After Who Took Utopia? *we did go to a studio in Bridgeton to start work on another project with the previous line up. I think we recorded three tracks but this song, without even hearing it again, used to be a random earworm that kept coming to mind. That project was scrapped but I kept asking Robbie if he had the stems and eventually he got them to me about seven years later. The song is so old that I can actually enjoy it. Vocals hadn't yet been recorded but drums, bass, guitar and keys were all there and sounding glorious. I didn't change any of the words, just used a live version as guide track and did less. In the live version, when we played Declan Welsh's EP launch, I was doing too much so I did less. And let the song tell the story. There was some additional mixing and production from Hamish at* Sound Sound *who did a great job of balancing Jo and my singing but it just feels like an audio capsule frozen in time and am so happy to have brought the old team back for one final song together in this project.*

FUN FACT: The sample at the end was David Lynch talking about catching ideas that you love and that takes us nicely into the next song which is called The Catch.

THE CATCH

Dimly lit scheme
Cause ae council skulduggery
So busy it's not funny
Dizzy, spun and fuzzy
Brought down to earth?
I was round-house kicked (well-founded)
Getting punched about once per month helps me keep
    well-grounded
Overall I'm more well-rounded
(rip up the subconscious with the odd knockout)
bless thyself with wisdom
(to maybe shut up about stuff we don't know much about)

Still chase the dunt of joy
That may make me naive
And I know that dreams are mental but I still choose to believe

    Catch a dream you're out your depth
    With a Fisher Price fishing net
    Welly boots up to your neck
    Get those feet under the desk

We are here for what is next
We are here for what is next
We are here for what is next

My will is built of a paper straw man
Tough to tell these days who is truly in yer corner
I stood up for the few, I flew into the eye
I rescued dog from fire, so today well why can't I?

The Sirens saw through my ear lobes with a nee-naw
PTSD ADHD OCD see-saw
As hard as U try today, I can't even leave the flat
Foot landlocked by the landlord in a tidal wave of panic
A psychic spike of heart-beat palpitations
But how can I complain when bombs reign down on nations?
The perfect early sunrise conceals a bloody mess
A bright dot in the sky bringing bread or certain death

> Catch a dream you're out your depth
> With a Fisher Price fishing net
> Welly boots up to your neck
> Get those feet under the desk

We are here for what is next
We are here for what is next
We are here for what is next

Gallop, I shall gallop, watch me gallop away
Gallop, I shall gallop, watch me gallop away
Gallop, star jump, gallop, see me gallop away
Gallop, I shall gallop, watch me star jump away

I remember rewriting this so much that there is a chance I unwrote it and made it worse than it was. Like a lot of these songs the general structure and melody was written at Carlton Studios with Teeth but then the days leading up to recording I wasn't sure if it was too personal or too vague which is a bad place as a writer as I wanted it to be both. I wanted to touch on certain subjects that hadn't been on the album yet but I didn't want it to look like something it wasn't. This was definitely the toughest session out the lot for personal reasons and I didn't believe the rest of the band when they said it was good. I still don't fully either but it has been validated by people who are usually very comfortable with telling me when they dislike a thing I've done. It felt like it was missing something and we tried a few things in post-production with different instruments that never worked. I think having Lily of Post Coal Prom Queen *adding the vocals really saved this one as I did think about deleting it completely. We also managed to avoid punk pop by the skin of our teeth by introducing certain elements. Then Ants from* Mickey 9s *asked if he could do a Popo Cops remix. I thought that would be class because I love that Scottish bam electro thing he does but he ended up doing a pop punk remix, and because he is far better at online promotion it has been the top song on our streaming platforms for the last year. So anyone, who goes to check out our band sees his remix first. How many fans have we lost? And how many have we gained? I guess we will never truly know but it IS definitely funny especially since we had to work really hard to avoid pop punk in this album. I completely missed that era. I confuse it with EMO. I don't hate it, I just don't understand it.*

The chatter at the end is a hot mic moment after I accidentally said 'star jump away' instead of 'gallup away'. It wasn't meant to be like that. I wanted to change it and delete the talking bit but I was voted down by everyone else in the room.

FUN FACT: The line 'the bright dot in the sky conceals a bloody mess' also has a sweary version. Hamish is so good at production that we recorded both versions at the same time. The only down side was being live on Sunny G *with Steg G as he played an exclusive premiere and I had to wait for that bit to make sure it was labelled correctly. The only swear on this whole album and I didn't even use it in the book because after much thought 'bloody' sounds better .*

IT FELT LIKE THE END

Fucking right! I'm miles away
Hand on window kinda day
I'm still in... I can't say
I bet I wake up far away
Last place you'd expect me tae
I'm still in... I can't say

I wish I could be more normal for you
Suitably goosed looking through a lucky horseshoe
The things that sort you sort of hurt you
And a piece of that pie is a cut above you
First there was light then there was two
Then three words said that self-combust you
Trust you to think out loud now she don't trust you
Honesty's a neat theory but in practice it's not good
Flirting with the truth and it flustered the costume
Blurting out stupid stuff that come back to haunt you
Is it lust? Is it love? Do I need you or want you?
Head hurts, damn burst, abandon the cartoon
Smart moves for us vanished into a dark room
Process negatives, snap the void in the vacuum
Plans cause for alarm, lack of harmony harms you
Come down to the calm bit, imagine the sand dune

Still on the journey to be the best me
Obstacles on the road seem to be here to test me
You can't make an omelette without breaking some eggs
You can't flee the nest without ditching common sense
A petulant pest with questions for my friends
They would rather pretend that am back on the mend
Prevailing with lips shut that would be telling

Silence says it all, it is literally telling
Yelling at a red light I'm not angry
Late for the funeral, am a daftie
Best-laid plans end up quite badly
And I can be as savage as I used to be sadly
Yelling at a red light I'm not angry
In the passenger chair, taxi driver stares blankly
I'm still in... I can't say

So I lied about having no more swear words, forgot about this one. I wrote this just days before a global pandemic and lockdown distracted us from everything. A few months later I was at Gordy's flat listening to his never-ending vault of unreleased music and I loved this beat instantly. He said he had hit a brick wall with it and I tried this poem over it. Sometimes I think the first take was the best version of it but it was ruined by a few minor mistakes and the fact I was singing 'Heaven Knows' instead of 'fucking right'. The thing I have learned is that if yer gonna make what sounds like a nice, stereotypical, poppy love song of heartbreak then you should always add a massive swear on the hook so you don't end up with any accidental radio play. It took so long to sign off on the final mix because it still felt lacking. Not even a well-placed swear word could fix it completely. At one point the great producer Dominic Hawken who produced Can I Kick It *by* A Tribe Called Qwest *and co-wrote* Stay Another Day *by* East 17 *was wanting to work on it. Sadly he passed away, he seemed like a lovely guy, and I had enjoyed our chats over lockdown. Konchis aka Jetsam then stepped up to the plate and gave the song more bass and an overall brighter sound and then Morphamish gave it a final tweak and master so it would blend in with the rest of the album.*

I also want to shout out Martin Windebank for filming me over two years every time we both ended up somewhere rural and it's weird watching it back because I write this right now from 'the last place you'd expect me tae.'

THIS NOT CIRCUS

Swirling whisky for the tooth decay
The highlight of my day
The persistent migraine all but swallowed away
I disintegrate, sway, turn grey then wallow away
Lost in a maze meant that I follow a stray

I know what it looks like but it's not circus
I swear down, with this clown, as my witness
Just a mild turbulence (and a question of fitness)
Coz it's not, this not circus

The best thing about losing everything is nothing
Nothing!
You got nothing to lose
The best thing about losing...
Trust me, trust me, trust me, trust me
The best thing about losing everything is nothing
Nothing!
You got nothing to lose

Chimpanzee do tricks
For reward or punishment
But keep your furry mitts, off the prize, encouragement
Is what's needed and prescribed
Shopping-mall malnourishment
An extortion on the surface with
Product placement purchase

I don't work here anymore—
But this not circus
An elephant in the room is none of your business
That tiger to yer blindside up to mischief?
It's a coincidence
This not circus

The best thing about losing everything is nothing

We got roadmaps and satnavs
And catnaps with caveats
Stats about addiction, stabbing Scotland's dark past
They have pie charts, and wall graphs
And cashback cause they killed the arts
Exit through the gift shop windae
Fish swimming through the trolleys and the shopping bags

The best thing about losing everything is nothing

Go for the juggler / jugular!

The first verse was an unused out take from Late Night Sketchy. *The song name* This Not Circus *was a title I had in my head since the scrapped EP that followed immediately after* Who Took Utopia? *There are various nods to older material throughout. The last verse was written there and then as I didn't like what I had originally recorded. I'm pretty sure I was hungover and full of self doubt. As usual vocals come at the end so it can be a long day of decision-making and questioning your life choices. The rest of the band are not used to waiting about as much so by me making changes, a bored Jo D'arc suggested doing a fast / loud bit at the end as an ode to* The Giros *which turned out really well. We were on a strict deadline of x amount of studio sessions to release the album in time so cancelling / postponing was not an option. Not even when Gordy called a sickie. Jess called Marcel who did these drums live after hearing the song for the first time. He did a great job and the synth sounds perfect. Morphamish really gave the full song the kick it needed.*

The end samples are Carl Jung discussing serendipity and coincidence then it switches to our friend Clare Campbell who was one of many people who sent voice notes of their dreams. It's sad that most were left on the cutting room floor. We had to leave most of Clare's out too as the initial mix including her full five-minute anecdote of recalling what happened in a vivid dream. We nearly kept it all in but realised we had been in the studio for too long and needed sleep. Which is a nice segeway to the next one Steal My Sleep.

STEAL MY SLEEP

Dishevelled guys, severed ties
Now they're bevvied pies, same path as I
Phone cameras die so there's no reply,
And no proof of why but I, I, I know
Lonely shuffle without structure
Gut-wrenching, lung-puncture
Wires in the cloud to solve the puzzle
Electrical wires in the eyes, the seas, the bees, in trees, in trouble

> It's been a long summer
> Been a long summer
> It's been a long summer
> Been a long summer

Please, please sell me autumn leaves
Or a blast of winter so I can breath
The sums of my sins multiply
Digging myself deeper, trying to make it right
The guilt builds so steep it reeks
It kills me daily, steals my sleep
And drops me off at the deep end

> It's been a long summer
> Been a long summer
> It's been a long summer
> Been a long summer

Jo and myself were in a sleepy village called Tapozlam, about an hour outside Mexico City, and we played a few songs on a live stream for You Call That Radio. *The guitar was out so we decided to get a jam as we had agreed to play a set in* Dash the Henge *record store in Camberwell, London on our way back to Scotland. We thought it would be good to try out something fresh so I looked through voice notes of the jam we had when we showed her the songs myself and Mark had been working on. And one of them was that bass line that Jo brought to the table. It was a rough recording with just bass and vocals, but it actually sounded decent. It had been a long summer for many reasons. I didn't need to change any words. For whatever reason that bass line and that random page of lyrics just went together from the very start and no changes were made to the song. Naturally, drums, guitar and synth were added later to give it a build but practically zero effort went into the writing of this one. Some songs take ages, some just appear out of the thin air. It's been a joy to play at festival season. It's nice, slow and easy for me. Deliberately well-placed in the set list to give me a break before the grand finale. I also want to give credit to Jenny on drums who has given so much dedication to her craft over the last couple of years whether onstage or in the studio depsite it being a very, very long summer.*

FAT ELVIS TIME

The volume and the colours were a lot today
So I took away my pain with a takeaway
Painkiller for my cranium? Not today
But I missed the train coz am a mystery
So I try to catch a bus but not today
The votes are in and the bots were paid
Should've walked away but not today
I will die one day mate but not today

> Born with a spade to DIY an early grave
> I was born with a spade to DIY an early grave
> Some were born with a silver spoon yet never made the grade
> I was born with a spade to DIY an early grave

Have you ever sold a pub out? Not today
A day when DIY became DOA
Where the hell has my band went anyway?
Still angry but nae energy
I flyered the polis, gang aft aglay
The barmaid and the bouncers bolted away
I should've followed them but am OK.
DIY? OK! Dae it anyway

> Born with a spade to DIY an early grave
> I was born with a spade to DIY an early grave
> Some were born with a silver spoon yet never made the grade
> I was born with a spade to DIY an early grave

...and is if by magic, Teeth finally gets his first guitar solo. I am not totally against guitar solos but am very opposed to the formulaic nature in which some bands just do it for the hell of it near the end of every song, a notion that Jo clearly agrees with too. I appreciate my guitarist's patience and understanding because if I could play guitar like him I would probably never not be doing solos. I would solo while shopping at a supermarket. It is a well-deserved solo for all he has given to the band both in this project but especially the live performances especially the sketchy ones early on when we weren't going in any coherent direction. I think recording this at Sound Sound *may have been my favourite moment as we had Teeth, Jo and Jenny Tingle doing the backing vocals at the chorus and when you mute the music it sounds like it could be a* Meatloaf *song. Morphamish did bounce a version that ended with the a capella but it sadly ruined the narrative of the album. Hopefully there is a remix somewhere that may see the light of day at some point.*

The ending would eventually be Josephine Sillars replicating that voice note that I sent to all my keys players that we spoke about during We Need an Intro *to tie it all together. Morphamish masterfully integrated Howdo Bean's piano in the background by slowing it down and adding some secret ingredients. It's good to see that melody that I wrote as a kid get not one but two appearances on the record.*

A LIGHT AT GLASGOW CENTRAL

I'm with my dead best friends running in slow motion
They sedated me
Went to the moon on ma own, cracked a shot off the cross bar
Missed ma penalty
Armed with a dart in the dark for an elephant rampant
On the motorway
Satellite dish twists just a ghost on the radio
Change the frequency

ooooh aaaah
ooooh aaaah

Give a man a fish and it turns into blimp
Manifest a wish, flick the switch and shift to if
All I want right now is just to lay here
And stay here forever and...

Give a man a phone and he turns into a drone
Remembering everything to forget you're on your own
I wish I was just enough to be me
To live here
To lay here
To stay here forever and one more tune

Stop
Go
Stop
Go

I woke up at Central on the Hope Street exit
They sedated me
Saw a lookalike like me but a younger version
He seemed scared of me
I asked for a light but there was no light there... yet
He just dingied me
Tried to warn him about the future but I'm slurry and sleepy

and the toon was deid
and my battery..

I knew we needed an ending. I was obsessed with how to do that. If you remember Who Took Utopia? *ended with all guns blazing on* Escape! Routine!, *a slow build with an emphatic finish. That was in my head for this song. I could hear the melody, the words and almost a full orchestra behind it so went to Gordy's to explain the song. He picked up the acoustic and played this. We recorded it in the first take to go away and make changes. I rewrote it and sent it to an incredible singer / musician Sev Ka to see if she had any ideas to improve it. She responded with 'leave it alone. It's fine as it is' and around that same time something happened that made me realise I didn't have time to re-record and add all the bells and whistles. We had already missed our deadline and it was time to wrap it up. Despite the fact I had wasted time rewriting it and despite the fact I can hear mistakes in this version. There is something fitting about ending a* Giros *album with an imperfect one-take demo. Just myself and a friend trying to figure something out with one microphone and one acoustic guitar. Back to where it all began. We never got fame, we never got money, but this band opened up so many doors and took me on more adventures than I could ever have dreamed of and that's why dreams are mental. Enjoy the journey.*

Dreams are Mental

But we still dare to dream, we make plans and try to achieve things beyond our grasp in a physical realm. Even if it sets you up for disappointment. Sometimes you question the point in even bothering and you think dreams are mental to even have.

Dreams are mental.

When you sleep and you dream you can fly every night. Wake up thinking dreams are mental by the way.

Dreams are mental.

They say dreams are mental, emotional, or sensory experiences that happen to us when we lose our grip on reality. But what happens when reality is mental?

There are three ways to comprehend the Dreams Are Mental *title. There is three Es in the phrase. Every album I have ever made, with* Girobabies, Jackal Trades *or other projects, have three word titles. Three is the magic number as we progress to what is surely the last ever* Giros *album. A long time had passed in between this and the previous record. We did still tour and play festivals. We did still record and release singles but it felt like we were once again back to having a high turnover of band members until another Mark aka Teeth joined the band on guitar. At first, he was just nailing the classics but for this to work we had to make an album or I didn't want to do it any more. I don't want to wing it on nostalgia and feel like a tribute band. So we met three times at Carlton Studios in three weeks and wrote three songs in each session. Once we had nine songs we invited Jo D'arc along to give her honest opinion (she doesn't do alternatives to honest opinions) and were relieved to hear she liked them too and even threw in a bass line of her own for a 10th song. Some tunes made the final cut and others were replaced but we had an album in theory and my good friend, collaborator and a guy who helped me turn* You Call That Radio's *audio podcast into a live video stream Morphamish seemed keen to get us into the studio. I respected him as a techno DJ/ producer and loved working with him as* Jackal Trades *but was initially cautious about bringing the band into* Sound Sound *studios until he started playing drums in front of me and explained he started in a punk band. That was enough for me and so we made an album called* Dreams Are Mental. *Artwork by Martyn Nuey. You should know him by now.*

THE GIROBABIES

SOCIAL NOT WORKING

Released 15 August, 2010
All songs written by: M. McGhee/ J. Hayes (except track 2 *What could Go wrong?* which was M.McGhee/ R. Gunn)
Features performances from: M. McGhee/ J. Hayes/ M. Yuen/ S. Andrews/ R. Gunn/ J. Hopkins
Produced by Stephen Scott, Elba Studios, Glasgow (except track 5 *Time Machine Prescription* which was R. Gunn)
Artwork by Jerry Dowds at punk-art.co.uk

BUS STOP APOCALYPSE

Released 5 June, 2012
Most tracks produced by R.Gunn (except track 2: S. Higgins)
All tracks written and performed by The Girobabies
2,3,4,9: M.McGhee/ J. Hayes
1,6,7, 8: M.McGhee/ R. Gunn
5: M.McGhee/ J. McCrory

WHO TOOK UTOPIA?

Released 28 September, 2015
All songs written and performed by M.McGhee/ R. Gunn
featuring additional performances by Gordy Duncan, John McCrory and Jo D'arc
Recorded in various studios and flats
All songs produced by Robbie Gunn and mastered by Green Door Studios
Artwork by Martyn Yuen
Vinyl released by Grebo Records

DREAMS ARE MENTAL

Released 19 August, 2025
Recorded by Morphamish at Sound Sound Studios (except 8, 12 recorded by Gordy Duncan, 5 recorded by Fionnbharr Marshall, 6 recorded by Robbie Gunn)
All then mixed and mastered by Morphamish with track 8 featuring additional mixing from Konchis aka Wav Machine.
All songs written and performed by The Girobabies, mostly by Mark McGhee and Mark McKeown except:
1: Howdo Bean / Mark McGhee
6: Robbie Gunn/ Mark McGhee
8: Gordy Duncan / Mark McGhee
10: Jo D'arc / Mark McGhee
12: Gordy Duncan/ Mark McGhee
All lyrics by Mark McGhee
Artwork by Martyn Yuen
Vinyl distribution by Paul McCabe

Thank you to everyone involved in making this album possible. Thank you to all band members past and present. Thank you fans, friends, and family. I would also like to thank Jenny Tingle, Mima Merrow, Josephine Sillars, Helea Gimeno, Alan Gray, Claire Campbell, Marcel Moliner, Jess Aslan, Alan Gray, Calum Cummins, Izzy Flower and Colin McCafferty their contributions. Shout outs to Hazy. This album was powered by the patreons of *You Call That Radio*. Dedicated to the memory of Robert McGhee.

WE NEED AN OUTRO

I don't know why we do it ourselves. The time, the effort, the cost and the anxiety to share ideas to an audience who only sometimes cares. But we are engulfed in the touring band loop. I am currently on an Irish tour just a few hours before the book deadline and thought I would add some final thoughts. On Friday night, my band had to play a show without me because someone decided on a whim that I didn't have sufficient ID. High on her power, she enjoyed telling me that there was no way I was going to Ireland. Of course, I still went to Ireland, but I had to go a different, longer route meaning I missed the first of five shows. For a few horrible hours my world seemed to crash around me and I decided that I was done. Then last night, in Dundalk, everything was perfect so I look forward to Derry tonight. But the loop is not as straight-forward as that. A bad show will make you want to redeem yourself and a great show will make you want to repeat it. When something goes well then we sleep off the self-belief we created so we can live the next day in fear. I know exactly what it takes to 'make it' and giving your everything is not enough. This band is now old enough to buy a pint and I think has come to a logical conclusion. I will pour my sacrifices and sufferings into writing a novel or take up painting until I inevitably start a new band that feels better and fails better. This is a partial strike of zero importance. The music industry is a pyramid scheme where you need immense wealth to pay for a sufficient amount of smoke and mirrors to baffle the general public.

It is a privilege to write but it is mainly pain management. Sometimes the therapeutic scribbles can slay demons. At the very least, a pen on a page can bare weight of fatigued shoulders.

All that is written should eventually be spoken out loud with select works being cast in iron with a ritual known as repetition. On days like today, others are spoken first before being translated into text. While most are quickly discarded others are memorized by small groups of people who then perform the new muscle memory ceremonies known as 'concerts' where a congregation gathers to critique or celebrate the works.

The congregation grows, as does the pressure. You need a team. I have no team. There has never been any help offered that I was stupid enough to accept. If you offered to manage me, I refused because I was unwilling to manage you.

I don't know why artists do any of it. I can only conclude that is a primal urge as there is no rational reason to pour your heart and soul out to the world simply to be judged, mocked and even stalked. The ability to write saved my life and got me to do things beyond my wildest delusions. We sang, we danced and we shared beautiful moments that I would never change. Sometimes waves of gratitude overwhelm me when I'm given space to reflect. I wish I could stick that feeling in a jar for the darker days. I wish I could freeze that first exhale from a cigarette after escaping a sweaty sold-out venue and finally feeling the cold air of relief mixed with the adrenalin starting to fizzle out. Being in a band saved my life and ruined my life at the same time. The plan you set yourself is always shifting as the goal posts move. The allure of something else will appear. There isn't an end-level boss to defeat. You will never be happy. All I wanted was to record a song then play a festival then it was play Europe. Since Dundalk is still in the EU that will need to count so I can have closure.

All success stories are vastly exaggerated: at best life will always carve out lottery winners here and there to fill you with a kernel of hope and a slice of resentment.

If you look at the globe from a telescope, we are self-destructive fungus which figured out cheat codes for temporary joy. There is a tribal yearning to be understood. Music and books do exactly that, but I doubt that any artist really knows what the hell they are doing. Everyone is winging it for joy or money. Validation or applause. Free drugs or status. But I think the majority are simply tapping into an inherent compulsion that they have very little control over. How can artists be credited for anything when they are doing exactly what anyone would do if they had shared the same genetic structure, identical brains and consumed the exact same culture? All creations are a reflection on the company you keep, the upbringing you had and the way you process and interpret new information, old emotions and other people's creations. It's trapped in DNA, written in stars and, as if by magic, sometimes appears in paperback books.

Mark McGhee
2026

ALSO AVAILABLE FROM SALAMANDER STREET

All Salamander Street plays, poetry and lyrics can be bought in bulk at a discount for performance or study. Contact info@salamanderstreet.com to enquire about performance licenses.

MINERVA AND THE WHIR by Jo D'arc
ISBN: 9781838403614

'The act of taking human form is not for the faint-hearted.' Jo D'arc's magical text takes the reader on a journey across the elements as Minerva wakes and explores the earth.

RAFFERTY'S RULES by Frank Rafferty
ISBN: 9781738429363

Glaswegian-born, Derry-based performance poet Frank Rafferty shares his comic musings coupled with political calls to action.

UNDER THE SUN OUR HEARTS ARE BEATING by Seki Lynch
ISBN: 9781739103040

Finding hope in the depths of disconnection, *Under the Sun Our Hearts Are Beating* is a gathering of consciousness, seeking to dissolve some of the invisible barriers between us.

HOPE IS A SILHOUETTE by Lana McDonagh
ISBN: 9781739103019

A body of intimate and introspective poetry with accompanying illustrations, both written and painted by Lana McDonagh.

O IS FOR HOOLET by Ishbel McFarlane
ISBN: 9781913630126

A solo show about the Scots language that challenges and disrupts our expectations and prejudices about language.

www.ingramcontent.com/pod-product-compliance
Lightning Source LLC
LaVergne TN
LVHW051645080426
835511LV00016B/2512